SABOTAGE

SABOTAGE

How to recognise and manage
employee defiance

*Dr Farhad Analoui
and
Professor Andrew Kakabadse*

MERCURY

Copyright © 1991 Farhad Analoui and Andrew Kakabadse

First published in 1991
by Mercury Books
Gold Arrow Publications Limited,
862 Garratt Lane, London SW17 0NB

Set in Meridien by Phoenix Photosetting

Printed and bound in Great Britain by
Mackays of Chatham PLC, Chatham, Kent

British Library Cataloguing in Publication Data
Analoui, Farhad
  Sabotage: How to recognise and manage
  employee defiance.
  I. Title   II. Kakabadse, Andrew
  658.3

ISBN 1–85251–059–5

CONTENTS

AUTHORS' NOTE

In order to conceal the identity of those involved, all names of organisations and their members have been changed.

For the sake of clarity alone and unless the text indicates otherwise, the term 'he' will include members of both sexes.

INTRODUCTION

Traditionally, managers have been primarily occupied with two major concerns. Firstly the achievement of their firm's objectives, and secondly the elimination and avoidance of conflict within their organisation. The history of early industrialisation is rich with accounts of unconventional practices such as sabotage, absenteeism and low productivity. Unfortunately, owners and managers did not or would not interpret these practices as attempts on the part of their staff to express resentment at the ways in which they and their work activities were managed. Instead, behaviour such as absenteeism was seen to be evidence of an individual's 'bad' character and strikes and sabotage were said to be criminal. Every schoolchild worth his salt knows what happened to the Luddites in the nineteenth century, and to the striking coal-miners and mill-workers in later days, to name but a few. Even those individuals who had the temerity to voice different opinions from those of the managers were said to be 'troublemakers'.

Some attempts were made by academics to point out that at least some undesirable practices in the workplace could be regarded as the result of discontent. But these were largely ignored. The theoretical and ideal view of the workplace populated by individuals all working together in harmony to achieve the organisation's goals persisted. Those who did not fit into this picture because they broke machinery or absented themselves from the workplace could be accounted for by being described as immoral. These miscreants could then be dismissed, jailed, sent to the colonies or hanged (at least in earlier days). The God-fearing owners and managers could then rest assured that justice had been done and sleep with an easy conscience – at least until the next time there was 'trouble at t'mill'.

In 1966 the renowned industrial sociologist Alan Fox advocated that a different managerial philosophy should be adopted. The workplace should not be seen as one which contains a united collection of people all working towards the same set of organisational goals, but as a place in which each individual pursues his own goals and interests. Fox argued that when these different interests conflict it is then that strikes and so on will occur. In other words, strikes, sabotage and similar practices can be seen not simply as acts of collective mutiny but as ways of expressing discontent – discontent which has been caused either directly or indirectly by the inevitable differences of interest which exist between managers and employees.

Fox's pluralistic theory and his view of conflict was widely accepted and acclaimed. At this point in history it could be seen that a great step forward had been taken. At last it was being recognised that the saboteur, the striker, the absentee and so on were people who actually had a grievance. However, while Fox was being hailed for his brilliant insights into the workplace, organisation theorists were still working on very simple models of Man as an employee. For example, one enduring idea in the history of organisation theory was that we should regard the employee as a machine, a mechanism who only responds to what is said to him or what happens around him, but who does not think for himself or act on his own initiative. It has also been argued that the best way to look at Man in the workplace is as an 'economic being', interested . only in what his wage packet will bring.

From the seventies onwards and especially in the late eighties, some management specialists, psychologists and behavioural scientists attempted to provide managers with alternative lenses with which to examine their organisations, people and work relationships. As a result a more realistic view

2

began to emerge. This invited us to regard people in the workplace as political agents who were capable of consciously defining, redefining, interpreting, regulating and imposing their own definitions of reality on others and situations.

However, although it was implicitly agreed amongst academics that people do have the potential for autonomy and that some forms of behaviour such as strikes and absenteeism can be explained as choices made by the aggrieved to express their discontent, relatively few attempts were made to explore the nature of these actions. As a result, we still did not know why there was discontent in the workplace. The attempts which have been made to explain this have largely centred around the theme of resistance and control. Strikes and destructive practices were seen, for example, as attempts on the part of the employees to resist the power of the management and to exert some control over their own work. Others have seen these practices as the workers' response to the oppression of work. These are certainly valid ways of looking at this intriguing subject. However, they do remain curiously impersonal explanations and create more questions than they answer.

The workplace of today is very different from that which could be found in early industrialisation. The factory employee will no longer cower at his work-bench as the overseer walks by, stick in hand, ready to clout him if he is not working hard enough. He will no longer burn the factory down because he is being paid starvation wages and in desperation sees no other choice *but* to burn the place down. In this shining new world of the late twentieth century, employees are truly fortunate in comparison. If they have a grievance they can take it to the management, in person or through the shop steward or some similarly elected or appointed personage. Today there are institutionalised procedures through which employees can make their feelings known and have their problems resolved. But they do not always take this option. Instead they may go home with their pockets full of paper-clips, office stationery in their bag and some of the petty cash in their shoes. It is recognised that the workplace is chock-a-block with unconventional goings-on. Pilfering, rule-breaking, destructive practices etc. abound there. It is even conceded that such behaviour can be employed to express discontent, to get even, but the question is *why*? Why do people employ such behaviour to get even when most organisations have laid down recognised and institutionalised means of conflict-resolution?

A number of attempts have in fact been made to account for these forms of behaviour. Some anthropologists, sociologists and organisational theorists have described such behaviour as *deviant*. This, of course, poses the problem of 'What is deviance?' And the answer seems to hinge on the way the issue is approached. It can, for example, be argued that a practice cannot be described as deviant if the individual concerned does not see himself or the act as deviant. The behaviour itself may even become integrated into normal life and become acceptable. For example, the shop assistant in the bakery who regularly takes home bread, cakes, pastries and rolls may see this as a perk of his job, his right, and not as stealing from his employer. In turn, the employer who knows that the assistant is behaving in this way, but allows it to continue because it is cheaper than paying a better wage, can in effect be seen as condoning this practice. The question of what behaviour is deviant is thus obviously fraught with problems, and the notion of deviancy certainly does not provide an adequate explanation of why people decide not to employ existing institutionalised channels of conflict-resolution in their workplace.

In fact, to date, while organisation theorists have offered some valuable insights into these undesirable practices in the workplace, their explanations have not been wholly satisfactory. This is because the theorists normally adopt one of two main perspectives, either of which can only provide a partial explanation; they divide themselves between the 'objective' and 'subjective' views. Those writers who fall into the former and by far the larger camp tend to focus on the behaviour itself rather than on the individuals who are actually displaying it. Supporters of the 'subjective' view, the Social Action theorists, believe that people's behaviour at work can be wholly explained from the actor's own point of view. From this perspective there is little reference to contextual factors and to the presence of powerful influencing agents within both the workplace and the wider environment.

However, as pilferage, absenteeism and destructive practices etc. are evidently all detrimental to the organisation's well-being, it seems logical to suggest that if we knew more about these pernicious activities it might be possible to stem their flow; in other words to eradicate some of their causes and in turn not only have a better-motivated work-force but also save organisations and industry a great deal of money.

In order, therefore, to discover why people employ uninstitutionalised means to express discontent, to 'get even' at work, we decided on a multi-faceted approach as being the most productive. We believed that first and foremost one had to take into account the explanations of those involved, while also remaining objective enough to take into account the context within which defiant behaviour was displayed. To this end it was necessary to get close to and actually work with the staff and management engaged in undesirable behaviour emanating from their discontent. And this is what Dr Analoui did. In order to learn more about the ways in which people 'get even' at work, research data was gathered from a number of organisations. The authors' main source of material was the large and popular night-club Alpha. It was Dr Analoui's covert participation as an employee at Alpha which enabled us to achieve the objective of the research: to discover why people attempt to get even in ways which are not institutionalised. It took six years – 10,000 hours – of continuous fieldwork to produce the answers to our questions.

Undercover

Becoming accepted as a member of Alpha's social organisation proved to be a long, laborious and sometimes dangerous process.

The dangers of being sacked, of 'having his cover blown' or of being made redundant were ever-present.

Quite often the process of gaining information was carried out under difficult circumstances:

> After five hours in the semi-darkness, the heat and the noise of the club, we would all have aching feet, headaches, our patience would have been sorely tried several times by rude, drunk and impatient customers. We would be at the end of our tether and then I would see, for example, John put £5 into his pocket straight from the till. He doesn't look in the mood to discuss what he just did! When we were all tired and not in the mood for talking, a way of strengthening and affirming ties of friendship would be to pass round the mints. This I do and John relaxes. I tell him a joke while I'm doing it; he doesn't look quite so bad-tempered. At the punch line he laughs. Then I get him to tell me why he took the £5. He took it because he did not get a second break that night. None of us did, but John's upset about it because his mum's ill and he said he would telephone her on his break. With the £5 note he can get some flowers or chocolates to cheer her up.

Thus, slowly but surely, the complex processes of how and why people would use unconventional means to get even at work were understood.

It was discovered that there are two major categories of choices available to those who want to get even with others at work. They can choose the particular *action* they want to take, for example pilferage, and the *style* in which they want to take that action, for example on their own or in a group.

It was also discovered that in total there was a choice of six actions and four styles, which means that getting even can be done in *twenty-four* different ways.

Not only could acts of getting even be carried out in twenty-four different ways, a remarkable enough discovery on its own, but it was also found that these activities were not confined to the rank and file of employees. Managers were also found to experience feelings of frustration and discontent and to attempt to get even.

Further, it was discovered that while the choice of *action*, whether pilferage or destructive practices, can only tell us what has happened – for example, that a piece of machinery has been damaged – the *style* in which the action was carried out can tell us a lot more. These styles differed according to *who* was involved in the action (an individual or group), *how* it was carried out (whether openly or in secret), and *why* the action took place at all.

How the book is organised

In Part I, Chapter 1 an 'Involvement–Expression' model will be used to explain the criteria on which the four styles are based, namely *who? how?* and *why?* Following this the four styles – Lone Ranger, Sniper, Protester and Rebel – which can be employed to express defiance will be described. In Chapter 2, two questionnaires will be put forward. The first will be concerned with how far discontent is likely to emerge in your organisation, and its implications for you as a manager; the second will help you to determine which style you or others are likely to adopt.

In Part II of the book we shall explore the six different action strategies which have emerged as the means people can utilise to get even. These are Pilferage, Rule-breaking, Destructive Practices, Non-cooperative Practices, Disruptive Practices and Misuse. A chapter will be devoted to each of these actions. At the end of Part II, 'A review of key points' will identify the shared characteristics of the six different means of getting even. Comparisons will also be made between acts of getting even as expressions of discontent and more conventional modes of conflict-expression.

Part III will consist of one chapter, Chapter 9. In this chapter we shall put forward a comprehensive strategic package in which the creation of a Total Quality Service Culture will combat acts of getting even in the workplace by reducing both the need and the opportunity to get even.

Part I

1

STYLES

The style in which a particular action is carried out is the end result of several processes. The very first stage is concerned with whether or not discontent should be expressed at all. Once it has been decided that discontent *should* be expressed, certain criteria are brought to bear on the choice of action, namely *who* is to be involved, *how* the action is to be carried out and *why* it is to be carried out. So before embarking on a description of the four styles, we shall be concerned with exploring the who, how and why questions through the Involvement–Expression model. As we explore the dimensions of this model, Who? How? and Why? – the criteria on which the four styles are based – will be explained. But first of all we shall look at the initial stage of the decision-making process – which is whether or not discontent is to be expressed.

To express or not to express

Since discontent at work, as we observed, proved to be responsible for a large proportion of incidences of getting even, we have to differentiate between discontent as a subjective experience and the action which may or may not be taken as a result.

Discontent is the outcome of a series of experiences and emotions that are only discernible to others when discontent is expressed in a behavioural form. When someone does something displaying a grievance, can we deduce that that person is unhappy?

The differences between people and the dominant values held by them lead to inevitable clashes of interest in the workplace. Once it is realised that there is a difference of interest, the individuals involved – whether employee or employer – may or may not choose to express their discontent in a behavioural form. It is at this early stage that the individual will realise the degree to which his interests are compatible or incompatible with the interests of those with whom he works. Obviously, the greater the desire to achieve incompatible goals, the more likely it is that there will be feelings of discontent. These feelings of frustration, depending on how great they are, can provide a powerful stimulus to acts of getting even.

Detailed accounts provided by those people who have acted in order to get even indicate that more often than not, depending on how frustrated and discontented they feel, people carefully weigh up the alternative courses of action open to them and the consequences that their action may have for themselves and the party with whom they are in conflict. They then decide whether or not their frustrations should be expressed in terms of action.

Once an individual or group has decided that yes, there is a conflict of interest and that yes, they will take action, the next stage in this process is to decide how they are going to act and what they are going to do. However, the time taken to make the decision to express discontent may range from seconds to years. Some acts may be spontaneous – in the heat of the moment machinery may be damaged – or take some time to come to fruition, with those involved waiting for the right opportunity to present itself.

Once the decision to express frustration and discontent, to get even, has been taken the next important step is to decide in what way the action should be carried out. The results of these decision-making processes have led to the creation of four broad styles of getting even. The Involvement–Expression model demonstrates the criteria on which these styles are based. This model consists of three dimensions, as outlined below.

Involvement: Who?

Whether an act of discontent will be carried out by an individual or by a group will depend on whether the conflict of interest is seen as shared or unshared.

A group is defined as two or more people who share certain values, thoughts or beliefs concerning specific issues. Certain factors play an important part in determining whether or not action will be taken individually or collectively. Is the individual introverted or extroverted? Does he see others' values and beliefs as compatible or incompatible with his own? Do one or more individuals feel that action should be taken? That is, there may be a shared feeling of frustration over a certain incident, but only one person may feel sufficiently angry or discontented to take action.

Expression: How?

The decision as to whether an action is to be taken on an individual or a group basis is usually followed by the question of *how* the action should be taken. This dimension represents the two basic behavioural strategies which are available for expressing discontent – overt and covert. The distinction between overt and covert strategies is important, because it brings to the forefront the fact that people are not only capable of conscious selection of behaviour, but are also capable of explicitly planning behaviour to achieve particular objectives. More important, from the observations made in both service and manufacturing organisations, it became quite clear that individuals and groups would decide whether or not their action(s) and/or their identity was to be made known to the target. This is illustrated by the following two situations.

Brian:

Brian's girlfriend had brought her friends to the night-club for a drink. Brian, a barman, decided to take an unofficial break. Before he did so he poured out a round of drinks, triple Bacardis, triple vodkas and so on for himself, his girlfriend and her friends. He then went to sit at their table. Brian was in mid-flow, waving a cigarette around, telling his best joke, an arm around his girlfriend, when the Floor Manager approached the table and proceeded to give Brian a 'dressing-down' in front of his girlfriend and her friends. His main complaints were that Brian had left the bar when it was not break-time and that he was in a section of the club where he had no right to be.

Brian returned to the bar in a seething rage. 'That bastard! All right, I shouldn't have gone and sat with Liz and her mates but bloody hell, he didn't have to have a go at me in front of them. I'm going to get him for this.'

His friends did their best to calm him down and advised him not to do anything rash. When they pointed out that at least he had got away with the drinks he was somewhat mollified. He bided his time until Friday night. Towards the end of the session he went to the room where the ice-making machine was kept, ostensibly to get a bucket of ice. This he did, but when he came back he said, 'I don't like the look of that machine. I don't think it's working properly. I don't think we'll have any ice tomorrow. In fact I'm certain of it.'

When asked what he meant, he said, 'Now that would be telling, wouldn't it?'

At the beginning of the Saturday night session it was discovered that the ice machine was broken. At first this may seem quite a trivial matter, but if a night-club is unable to supply ice to its customers this can become more than just troublesome. Customers can become aggressive if they are not given an ice-cube in their drink. Men seem to regard it as an indictment of their manhood if they cannot return to their wives or girlfriends with the necessary pieces of frozen water floating in their drinks. If the bar staff cannot serve the drinks with ice they may not be given any tips. '*No ice*' can be a major disaster. The managers spent that particular Saturday night going round the nearby pubs and clubs requesting the managers to allow them to have some of their ice-cubes: a demeaning task, obviously, and Brian was able to feel that he had been successful in getting even.

Hilda:

Hilda, a cocktail barmaid, was sent to work on her own behind one of the smaller bars as a punishment for being 'too cocky'. The glass-washing machine behind that bar was broken and said to be not worth repairing. In order to ensure that Hilda should endure as much hardship as possible, the Floor Manager arranged for extra dirty glasses to be transferred to Hilda's bar – to be washed, of course, by hand. Hilda said that, like everyone else, she should only be responsible for washing her own share of glasses (those which originally came from her bar) and not everybody else's. When Tim, the Manager, retorted with a meaningful smile, 'Well that's how it is. What are you going to do about it?', Hilda paused for a moment and then suddenly threw a tray full of glasses into the bin and walked off the bar, collected her coat and went home.

The difference between these situations is clear. In Hilda's case, the action taken was meant to be observable and known to the target, whereas in Brian's case the target was not aware of the action taken against him until it was much too late; and Brian's identity as the perpetrator was also unknown. In other words it is possible to distinguish between those acts of getting even which are intended to be overt and those which are meant to be covert.

Overt strategy

Getting even by overt ways is probably one of the most well-known and popular strategies adopted by individuals and groups.

In situations where an overt strategy is employed, the intention of the aggrieved is to communicate and express discontent in an undisguised manner. It is intended that the action which is taken and the identity of the individual or group involved is to be known to the party against whom the action is taken.

Most routine and daily interactions at work take an overt form. Expressions of discontent like strikes, labour turnover, absenteeism, non-cooperation and even some serious destructive practices may all fall into this category.

Covert strategy

The covert strategy is used to disguise the identity of the perpetrators and/or the action that they take. This places them in a strategically advantageous position. The person(s) at whom the action is aimed will not know what has happened until it is too late. Equally, they will not be able to identify who was behind the action. Not knowing who the culprits are naturally makes it difficult to take appropriate disciplinary measures, which is precisely why this strategy is used. The more serious the repercussions are likely to be, the more likely it is that covert ways of getting even will be used.

Some actions invite more serious repercussions than others. For example, if minor rule-breaking is to be the chosen action, this will be done openly as long as it is almost certain that the consequences will not be serious. Generally, minor rule-breaking is not seen to be a serious misdemeanour and on a first occasion can be met with anything from a 'dirty look' to a reprimand, if not completely ignored. In contrast, the consequences of pilferage are more likely to be serious. A typical response can range from instant dismissal to prosecution. When such an outcome is possible, a covert strategy is usually preferred.

However, in situations where managerial domination is complete and any attempt to express discontent may have severe repercussions, a discontented individual or group may employ a covert strategy for any action.

Finally, even though the finer details of covert actions are usually planned and the outcome calculated, in some cases things can go badly awry: people can be caught red-handed or wreak more damage and havoc than they actually meant to. The following case is a good example of such circumstances.

The staff 'do'

A large insurance company had hired Alpha for its staff 'do'. It was known that it would be busy and all the club staff were asked to come in. A minute before the club was due to open, Tim, the Catering Manager, came up to the bar and told the bar staff that Chris, the bar supervisor, had telephoned to say she was too ill to come in. After he had gone Mandy, Ruth, Dave and Ali generally agreed that this was a 'likely story'. 'And it's packed outside. Did you see them queuing? How will we manage?'

They were most aggrieved and felt that Chris has let them down. But even while they were complaining it occurred to them that they now had an opportunity to get even. Chris would only have herself to blame if she was called to the office yet again with the other bar supervisors and lectured because of the stock shortages.

It was a busy night, and unusually large amounts of money were being taken on the bars. At eleven o'clock Tim came behind the bar and called everyone to him. 'Listen, I know you're up to your eyes but Mr Bond (the General Manager) is worried about all the money that must be in the tills, so we're asking you do to your tills one at a time and start again with a £25 float. Mandy, you start yours.' This had not happened before and was totally unexpected. To give herself and the others time Mandy started to count her money very slowly.

Tim, as he said later, thought that Dave was acting suspiciously and watched him out of the corner of his eye. When Mandy was counting her £10 notes for the fourth time Tim suddenly moved towards Dave and held his hands behind his back while he shouted, 'Go and get Mr Bond! Get the bouncers! Get the staff rep! Go on! Move! Get them!'

Once Tim had all the witnesses he needed he released Dave's hands and asked him to empty his pockets. He had £50 in different notes. Dave was asked to go up to the office and the bouncers, managers and the staff representative all left the bar.

Ruth was shaking with nerves. 'Oh God, what will we do? What if he says something?' When a glass-collector came and told them that the police had arrived she almost fainted. Mandy told her not to be concerned; Dave would not 'split' and while nobody would suspect them, it would be wise to dispose of any incriminating evidence. Just in case.

Dave was not the only victim on this occasion. Ruth was so upset by the incident that she relinquished her job at Alpha and security measures became so tight that it was said that 'You couldn't get away with a penny'. It was some time before the security measures were relaxed and it again became 'safe' to pilfer.

Covert strategies are thus usually adopted when the intention of the aggrieved individual or group is:

1. To protect the identity of those involved; or
2. To avoid the danger of the action being discovered; or
3. Both.

Motives and meanings

The third dimension of the Involvement–Expression model is fundamental to understanding what getting even is all about. We believe that people's actions are a reflection of their individual frames of reference, and that to understand why people take action it is necessary to explore underlying motives and meanings.

The meanings that people attribute to their actions can be divided into three main sub-categories: *personal, internal* (i.e. from within the organisation) and *external* (i.e. from outside the organisation). Of course, any one action can be due to a number of reasons, but in each case we took the major source of discontent at that time and for that action to be the main reason for attempting to get even.

Our research revealed that discontent emanated mainly from the interactions between groups and individuals, workers and managers within the work environment. Indeed, as many as two-thirds of the observed cases derived from an 'internal' source. However, if it had been known that discontent was brewing over issues in the workplace, most acts of getting even could have been avoided.

However, motives and meanings derived from outside the organisation were sometimes cited as the cause for action, and this reminds us that an analytical framework cannot be confined to workplace parameters. Obviously we need to recognise that the workplace and the world outside it are interrelated. It can be argued that the dominant socio-economic and political characteristics of a society influence and shape the ways in which both work organisations and those within them behave; and that discontent at work can be seen as rooted in the dominant value-structure of the society in which the organisation is placed. For example, in societies where the acquisition of material goods is considered important, workers in low-paid jobs will obviously feel discontented. That discontent will be aimed at those who do not provide them with the means of satisfying their material aspirations – in other words, their employers.

In the research, there were also cases where the reason for being discontented, upset or frustrated could not, with any real justification, be labelled internal or external, but were located in the personality and attitudes of the individual involved – for example, he might be ambitious. When the main cause of discontent could be attributed more to personality and attitudes of the individual than to the organisation or to external sources, we would say that the reasons for getting even were personal. In Part II, when we explore the six different actions which can be taken to get even, the motives for these actions will be examined more fully.

Now that we have explored the criteria on which people based their actions, we shall examine the four broad styles in which those actions could be taken.

The four styles: *modi operandi*

It was the choices made between individual or group action and acting openly or secretly that led us to realise that there are four different ways, four styles in which people can get even: they can adopt individual-overt, individual-covert, collective-overt or collective-covert action. It also seemed that over a period of time an individual would begin to show a preference for a particular style. Different styles would seem to suit different people and/or to be the most appropriate, as a rule, within a particular organisational context. Therefore the style chosen in order to get even conveys a great deal about an individual's dominant behavioural disposition. So much so that it was possible to label the four styles according to the sort of person who, as a rule, was likely to employ that particular style. We identified those who acted as *Lone Rangers, Snipers, Protesters* and *Rebels.*

Figure 1

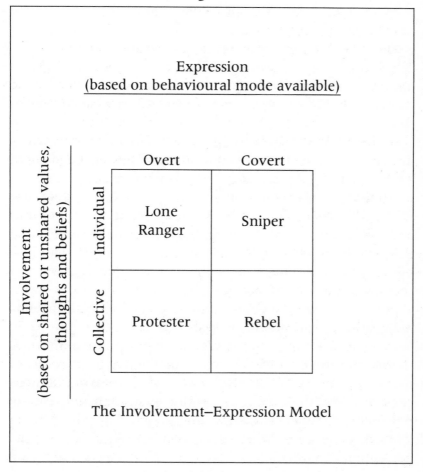

The Involvement–Expression Model

Lone Ranger

The Lone Ranger has usually been with the organisation for a long time. He strongly believes that the procedures for sorting out grievances at work are grossly inadequate. Such a view emanates from a belief that managers are not to be trusted. For the same reason the Lone Ranger rejects any attempts to institutionalise conflict further, to improve the existing system. A typical comment is that 'it won't work'. Obviously this means that the Lone Ranger regards work-related problems as insoluble, at least through normal channels. As a result the Lone Ranger keeps his problems to himself, in so far as the management is concerned.

The Lone Ranger also gives the impression that he is industrious. The unconscious need for recognition and approval from his colleagues and superiors can often induce the Lone Ranger to volunteer for extra responsibility, even though he does not particularly enjoy the work.

In the main, the Lone Ranger is highly independent. He is aware of his own interests and differentiates between them and those of the organisation. The Lone Ranger develops his own ideas and plans for changes and occasionally shares them with others, believing that his suggestions are the solution to any problems facing the organisation. However, the Lone Ranger's ideas are usually radical and are not met with any enthusiasm. The Lone Ranger then tends to feel rejected and sees his role as that of a crusader.

In fact the Lone Ranger is a loner. He does not make friends easily and he appears to be unable to trust others, probably because he feels misunderstood. In order to protect himself, therefore, the Lone Ranger will usually give the impression that he wishes to be left alone. And when the Lone Ranger consequently *is* left alone, it reinforces his belief that he is misunderstood. The lack of enthusiasm which meets his ideas when he does share them also tends to reinforce his self-perception as a loner.

When the Lone Ranger becomes frustrated enough to take action and to attempt to get even, he will usually take individual-overt action. Individual because of his loner tendencies, and overt because, despite the lukewarmness displayed by others when he does air his ideas, the Lone Ranger remains convinced that he is right.

Tom

Tom, a newly transferred assistant catering manager, could no longer hide the resentment that he felt against Franko, a well-established catering manager with twenty years' experience behind him. His transfer from a medium-sized branch to Alpha, one of the largest branches within IEC, was an opportunity for him to 'make it' in the company. Franko, aware of Tom's potential for promotion, felt threatened. He was heard to say, 'He can forget it if he's after my job. He can take his degree in Business Administration or whatever and go back to Leicester where he came from. He's got it all wrong.'

The hostility between the two reached the point where Tom used to criticise Franko openly whenever there was an indication that he had failed to manage the branch's affairs efficiently. Eventually Tom discovered that Franko had been occasionally pilfering the money received for champagne at private parties by not ringing up the amount on a cash till. He raised this matter in a staff meeting and was asked by the General Manager to put it in writing, which he did. Content that he had finally proved to his superiors that Franko was ineffective and had been pilfering, he went on to suggest a new procedure for recording the sale of liqueurs and champagne on occasions when they were provided directly to party organisers by the Catering Manager.

A fortnight later, much to Tom's surprise, he was informed that he would soon be transferred to a bingo hall in Leicester.

This was a much less prestigious place in which to work and Tom was quite candid about his reactions to the transfer. 'I know why this has happened, but I'd do the same thing again. You have to do what's right, right?'

The Sniper

The Sniper is dangerous! He appears to be a gregarious animal and to respect authority. However, this is only a persona he has adopted in order to achieve his own objectives.

While the Sniper appears to be sociable and gregarious, he would actually prefer to act alone. The Sniper is a loner and does not possess any real desire to join groups. However, the Sniper has acquired the necessary techniques of successful social interaction because he recognises that there are benefits to be gained from operating in groups and from being accepted as a group member. For example, unlike the Lone Ranger, the Sniper longs to move up the promotional ladder and can begin to achieve his objectives by being accepted and regarded as a 'good sort' by his colleagues and superiors.

Like the Lone Ranger, the Sniper has lost faith in the system, if he ever had it, yet sees the achievement of the organisation's objectives as a necessary evil if his own unpublicised objectives are to be realised. He recognises the need to conform with the organisation's rules and procedures. The Sniper publicly acknowledges the legitimacy of authority and calls for an institutionalised approach to resolve conflict at work. Even this, however, will not usually be done directly. Within a particular group the Sniper will attach himself to the person who has the most extrovert characteristics and is known to be outspoken. The Sniper's approach is to make suggestions to this person or to seek his opinions on a particular topic and ask him whether or not he thinks that 'it's about time someone said or did something'.

The fact that the Sniper appears to be a sociable, law-abiding citizen means no one would expect him to attempt to get even, and it is this which makes him dangerous. But he does attempt to get even and he is much more ruthless than the Lone Ranger. His actions will usually be individual-covert. Indeed the only way the Sniper can express his discontent is by individual-covert measures. The Sniper has not shared his true feelings with others, hence he must act alone and in secret. He also typically adopts a covert strategy because he tends to take actions which, if discovered, could provoke serious repercussions. While the Lone Ranger may express his discontent by arriving late at work, the Sniper is more likely to go home with a £20 note in his socks or to be the last to leave an already shuttered bar and lock the door behind him, having left a tap on.

The tip-off

Adam, the Catering Manager, had called for a staff meeting to be held on Friday evening at exactly 7 p.m. (one hour before opening time). Apparently the six-monthly stock check carried out by auditors from Head Office still showed a significant shortfall instead of a surplus as Adam had expected.

At the meeting the importance of 'getting stocks right' in monthly inspections was spelt out in detail. Pouring out the wrong drinks for customers was said to be a major contribution to the loss of stock. Sheila, the cocktail barmaid, was particularly criticised for her 'Aussie way of doing things'. She was told to attempt to serve the right drinks, 'or else'.

Adam's parting words were to the effect that 'Some of you will find some money's been deducted from your wage packets this week . . . Now let's do some cleaning. We're a cleaner short this month.'

When this was met by a general protest, the staff were told that if they held any strong objections they did not have to continue with their employment. 'A phone call to the labour exchange is all that's needed to replace you lot, don't you forget that.'

That weekend, Sheila and two other bar staff found that their wages were short by £5. Adam was not prepared to discuss the issue any further: 'You've been told, there's no excuse for that sort of behaviour.'

Sheila was especially annoyed because she felt that Adam had been extremely sarcastic when she had tried to talk to him about it. 'G'day! You're wasting my time, Sheila.' On her way out, Sheila said to a close friend, 'I'll show him a "G'day" that he'll remember for good.'

Early one Saturday morning, Adam was stopped and breathalysed by the police when driving home from work and was found to be over the limit. His plea that he had only had a single vodka and Coke did not impress the officers. He was fined heavily and lost the use of his driving licence for one year. It soon became general knowledge that the police had been tipped off to look out for a man fitting Adam's description who was to be found drunk and driving a cherry-red Ferrari in the early hours of the morning.

We leave the reader to draw his own conclusions as to who tipped off the police and as to why Sheila should have seemed particularly pleased at Adam's misfortune.

The Protester

The Protester is happier doing things in concert with others rather than on his own. Joining others to form a group or working-party comes naturally to him. Once in a group, Protesters are inclined to share the dominant collective values and norms and abide by the accepted code of conduct.

As an organisation member, the Protester sees legitimate ways in which things could be improved, yet he will be bored by the process of detailed planning necessary to bring about the changed state. Nevertheless, the desire for recognition from immediate group members makes him feel obliged to remain with the group and to contribute to it.

While Protesters are critical of authority they do not feel confident enough to take action on their own. Protesters will therefore typically take collective action and do this openly. Protesters believe that there is safety in numbers and feel less threatened by possible repercussions. Protesters will also usually act in the name of a collective cause rather than an individual crusade. Moreover, Protesters will usually act on the basis of a shared common belief or opinion, and because of this their activities will usually be supported by those who are not actually involved. However, this can sometimes have repercussions which the Protesters have not predicted. Having agreed amongst themselves that they are right and knowing that they have the unconditional support of their colleagues who are not actively involved, they can forget that their superiors are not of a like mind.

Too few; too many: what the hell d'you want?

Five glass-collectors were summoned to the Manager's office. They were told that Lulu, the supervisor of the Ambassador Bar, had complained that there was a shortage of glasses at the busiest times of the evening. The five employees were accused of not endeavouring to carry out their duties efficiently and of not providing her with spirit glasses.

At one o'clock in the morning, Lulu was heard complaining to the Catering Manager that she now had *too many* glasses. The bar staff were in high dudgeon: 'We can't cope with washing them let alone serving people.'

But Lulu was not prepared to accept defeat. The situation continued for four nights until three barmaids confronted Lulu. The barmaids were not only disgruntled about having to wash more than what they felt to be their fair share of glasses; they were also annoyed because it was preventing them from serving as many customers as they would otherwise have done – they felt they were missing out on gratuities because the customers were unhappy about having to wait while the glasses were washed. 'We're not prepared to wash up glasses all night long and get nowt for it.'

When the glass-collectors heard the bar staff were not co-operating with Lulu, they stepped up their action. Lulu was faced with discontented subordinates on the one hand and grumbling customers on the other. Eventually, Lulu left the bar to seek out the Manager and complain about both the bar staff and the glass-collectors who had all become 'very difficult'. This only served to exasperate the Manager who obviously felt that it was Lulu who was being difficult. 'One day you're complaining of a glass shortage and the next of too many of them. What the hell do you want?' The glass-collectors were told by the Manager to 'cool off'.

The sin that Lulu had committed was to complain to the Manager about her colleagues. It is an unwritten law that 'thou shalt not grass on thy workmates'. As Lulu broke this commandment she got her just deserts.

The Rebel

The Rebel is a person who seeks recognition from others with whom he shares anti-establishment feelings.

Rebels do not, in essence, recognise the right of their superiors to authority and it is this attitude towards their employers which provides the core values to which the Rebels subscribe. Unlike the Protester, the Rebel does not see any hope for the organisation. This attitude manifests itself in a deep sense of pessimism. 'It's too late to change things in this place' is a common response to any positive ideas.

Rebels regard themselves as victims of the system. They also feel that institutionalised forms of conflict-expression are not to be trusted. In contrast to the Protester, the Rebel is a highly creative and efficient individual and the number of Rebels within a group is usually smaller than that of Protesters. Rebels are very much aware of the consequences of their actions and believe in detailed planning to achieve their objectives. Unlike the Protester and the Lone Ranger, the Rebel can effectively work on his own while remaining part of a collectivity.

Rebels concentrate their efforts on identifying the loopholes that make the system vulnerable to their actions. These attributes render Rebels the most difficult group to deal with.

Keep an eye on them

The owner and Manager of a reputable steakhouse suspected that the waitresses were 'fiddling', and the Manager asked Joseph the grill chef, Linda the Head Waitress and the barmaids to keep an eye on the waitresses. 'I know you and Linda don't always see eye to eye because she's a Jehovah's Witness and you belong to the Seventh-Day Adventists, but I've asked her and I'm asking you to let me know if you see anything suspicious. Right. By the way, use last week's steaks first. Cut off the edges [the light brown mould]. It'll be all right. Just use a bit more seasoning and hurry up. It's nearly opening time.'

Over the next three months the takings improved and the owner and Manager did not see the need to involve an undercover security firm – 'Thanks to Joseph and Linda's vigilance'.

Joseph, Linda and Sue the barmaid had obviously made a wise decision when they agreed to reduce the amounts which they had been 'pinching'!

Now that we have explored the four styles in which people can get even at work and the criteria on which they are based, the next chapter will be concerned with you, your colleagues and your organisation.

2

QUESTIONNAIRES

Managers in bygone eras were notorious for the unsophisticated techniques they used in order to get the best out of their work-force. Today, managers are expected to do more than just ensure by various means that people will 'behave themselves', 'buckle under' and 'get the job done'. The art of management has become more sophisticated and requires that managers should be able to *help* people modify their behaviour if it is not acceptable. Managers can only do this if they have a sufficient knowledge and understanding of their employees' behaviour. In other words they need to know how individuals will respond to certain situations in the workplace. Where attempts to get even are concerned, managers particularly need to be able to gauge how individuals will respond to conflictual situations.

The two questionnaires presented in this chapter will help to provide you with some insight into your employees' and colleagues' behaviour, if you wish to conduct a survey.

However, before we can begin to try to understand other people and to help them change their behaviour, we need to understand ourselves. But if we are unable to see how our actions are formed, why we behave in certain ways and why some of our actions may be regarded as unacceptable, we tend to feel helpless and even to experience feelings of intense guilt and despair. Self-condemnation is not uncommon amongst people who find themselves involved, as either perpetrator or victim, in getting even. But if we are able to understand our own actions, we can systematically begin to gain control over the self. The way to this lies through identifying the underlying factors that cause us to behave in certain ways.

Imagine a situation in which a factory manager is being harassed by his superiors because he has to make frequent requests for crockery and cutlery for the factory canteen. The new orders of cutlery have no sooner arrived than they disappear and the crockery is constantly being broken. The manager suspects that this is being done on purpose, but he cannot understand why. He feels alternately angry and depressed about the situation. In search of an answer he then fills in the two questionnaires given below. As a result of the first questionnaire he learns that discontent is not particularly rife in his organisation and from the second that he is a Lone Ranger – a person who voices unpopular opinions but who on the whole keeps himself to himself. This may come as something of a surprise to him. He knows that he is sometimes misunderstood but he sees himself as a humane person. So humane in fact that he has recently extended lunch-breaks by fifteen minutes and tea-breaks by five. When his employees objected he took it to be out of loyalty to the firm, as their wages would not be affected. The manager made this change because he believed that it would create a more contented atmosphere in the factory and that people would work more efficiently if they had longer breaks.

However, in the light of what he has learnt from the questionnaires he can now begin to question his own actions. Did he really extend lunch- and tea-breaks because he believed that the quality of work would improve? Or was it because of his unconscious need, as a Lone Ranger, for recognition, for approval from his work-force? As a result of the questionnaire he can also begin to suspect that it may be the defence mechanisms he deploys in interpersonal interactions that have prevented anyone coming to tell him what the problem is: that is, his staff see him as unapproachable. He then starts to talk to people about the problem over the broken crockery and missing cutlery. The work-force are mainly women. He finds out eventually that the women would prefer to leave the factory twenty-five to thirty minutes earlier, or come to work that much later, rather than have longer breaks during the working day. They have families and would welcome more time to spend with them. The manager can then put into force a shorter working day, for which in return his now approving employees will continue to produce the same amount and quality of work.

In short, the first requirement for managing others is the ability to manage ourselves.

In the following pages you will find two questionnaires. The first deals with the extent to which conflict and discontent are likely to occur in your organisation, the second with the particular style of behaviour – Lone Ranger, Sniper, Protester or Rebel – that you (or those to whom you have given the questionnaire) prefer to adopt at work. As we said, the styles that people adopt are not viewed solely in relation to acts of getting even. The way in which an individual may express discontent is part and parcel of his or her whole workplace persona. The second questionnaire could thus be used merely to provide you with some valuable insight into your behaviour at work. On the other hand, if you are or ever have been discontented at work, and have felt that you had no choice but to resort to unconventional practices, then this questionnaire may help you to gain some insight into *why* it happened. The lengths to which you have gone in order to express discontent are immaterial. You may have been late for work once ten years ago because the manager upset you the day before, or you may be habitually (and perhaps even literally) putting a spanner in the works. Whatever action or actions you may have taken, both these questionnaires should help you to reach a better understanding of your situation. For example, if, after completing the first questionnaire, you discover that your organisation is a breeding-ground for discontent, you may no longer feel quite so personally responsible for the fact that what goes on there drives you to distraction: you will be able to place your own behaviour in a much wider context. The second questionnaire could also help you reach a better understanding of the behaviour of other people in your organisation.

Finally, we suggest that when filling in these questionnaires you might like to put your answers on a separate sheet of paper, so that the original is available for future use.

Questionnaire No. 1
Your Organisation

As we said earlier, we discovered that getting even is more likely to occur in some work organisations than others. This questionnaire will help you to determine the extent to which discontent is likely to be a problem in your organisation. The questionnaire contains twenty statements. Read each carefully and allocate a score between 0 and 5 points to each according to how true you find the description to be of your own workplace. Try to be as objective as possible.

In my organisation:

1. The emphasis is on a strong and decisive leadership that expects unquestioning loyalty from its subordinates.

Not true   *Very true*
0 . . . . 1 . . . . 2 . . . . 3 . . . . 4 5

2. Managers tend to treat new ways of doing things with suspicion, especially if the idea comes from subordinates.

Not true   *Very true*
0 . . . . 1 . . . . 2 . . . . 3 . . . . 4 5

3. In my organisation it is believed that a good subordinate is one who is 'all for the organisation'.

Not true   *Very true*
0 . . . . 1 . . . . 2 . . . . 3 . . . . 4 5

4. Procedures are laid down for getting things done, but the boss may change the rules if it suits him, or when under pressure.

Not true   *Very true*
0 . . . . 1 . . . . 2 . . . . 3 . . . . 4 5

5. In my organisation it is continually said that no one, of any rank, is indispensable.

Not true   *Very true*
0 . . . . 1 . . . . 2 . . . . 3 . . . . 4 5

6. People at the top avoid responsibility and often pass the buck to subordinates. This is done under the guise of delegation and allocation of responsibilities.

Not true   *Very true*
0 . . . . 1 . . . . 2 . . . . 3 . . . . 4 5

7. Every so often someone is made a scapegoat for doing something that everyone else does, but which is not formally allowed.

Not true   *Very true*
0 . . . . 1 . . . . 2 . . . . 3 . . . . 4 5

8. The present procedures for handling grievances and conflict are lengthy and cumbersome. Even worse, people with a grievance are indelibly labelled as troublemakers.

Not true   *Very true*
0 . . . . 1 . . . . 2 . . . . 3 . . . . 4 5

9. There seems to be little commitment, especially on the part of subordinates and junior management, to the long-term objectives of the organisation. 'Getting by' seems to be the most favoured attitude.

Not true   *Very true*
0 . . . . 1 . . . . 2 . . . . 3 . . . . 4 5

10. Almost everyone is aware of the current difficulties with which the company is faced. These are often discussed, but are never communicated to the top. The argument is that 'no one is interested enough to take them on board'.

Not true   *Very true*
0 .... 1 .... 2 .... 3 .... 4 5

11. Individuals or groups are encouraged to use their initiative, even if it means bending the rules a little, to achieve the organisation's objectives. So long as nothing goes wrong, nothing is said; but if it does, they are blamed for not sticking to the rules.

Not true   *Very true*
0 .... 1 .... 2 .... 3 .... 4 5

12. The pay system is inadequate and unfair. Rewards are allocated through favouritism rather than according to competence.

Not true   *Very true*
0 .... 1 .... 2 .... 3 .... 4 5

13. People are primarily controlled by censure and punishment and motivated by pay and fringe benefits.

Not true   *Very true*
0 .... 1 .... 2 .... 3 .... 4 5

14. Employees' real interests lie outside the work environment; work merely provides a means to an end and is not the end itself.

Not true   *Very true*
0 .... 1 .... 2 .... 3 .... 4 5

15. Seniority is assessed by length of employment with the company rather than by how many courses you have taken. In reality formal qualifications are more of a handicap than an advantage.

Not true   *Very true*
0 .... 1 .... 2 .... 3 .... 4 5

16. Change is often talked about but rarely attempted. The middle management prefer the traditional way of doing things.

Not true   *Very true*
0 . . . . 1 . . . . 2 . . . . 3 . . . . 4 5

17. We seem to be always one step behind our main competitors.

Not true   *Very true*
0 . . . . 1 . . . . 2 . . . . 3 . . . . 4 5

18. There is a strong feeling of 'them' and 'us' between management and employees.

Not true   *Very true*
0 . . . . 1 . . . . 2 . . . . 3 . . . . 4 5

19. Most people within the organisation see their involvement as a job rather than as a career. What is more, the powers that be show little interest in the development of the individual and his or her future career.

Not true   *Very true*
0 . . . . 1 . . . . 2 . . . . 3 . . . . 4 5

20. No steps are taken to prevent problems from occurring. When problems do emerge, they are dealt with by 'firefighting' methods.

Not true   *Very true*
0 . . . . 1 . . . . 2 . . . . 3 . . . . 4 5

Total [ ]

How to interpret your score

Add up the scores. The total indicates the likelihood of people in your organisation resorting to getting even.

0–24

This score is representative of healthy work relationships, with a management which is aware of the need for effective two-way communication between themselves and their staff. The dominant managerial style can be characterised as 'selling' rather than 'telling'. This style has probably already encouraged innovation and a shared concern for efficient production and service.

Occasional disagreement will be dealt with promptly and constructively. Both formal and informal channels of communication are used to avoid the escalation of discontent. The causes of disagreements and possible conflictual situations, no matter how trivial, are taken seriously.

The likelihood that people in your organisation will resort to unconventional practices is relatively small. Discussion and negotiation in a friendly environment seem to be the order of the day and are routinely used to resolve differences. Occasional acts of non-cooperation and misuse may be observed but these are often attempted by new recruits who have not yet become fully socialised into the system.

The prevailing style for conflict-expression is overt, and while the danger of destructive practices is minimal, the management should not succumb to over-confidence.

25–49

This score indicates that differences between individuals and groups on both sides, management and staff, have led to the occurrence of 'accidents'. Institutionalised channels of conflict-resolution are viewed as inadequate or unworkable. The nearer your score is to 50 the more likely this is to be true of your organisation.

The established procedure for conflict-resolution is probably lengthy and time-consuming. The distance that is created between management and staff has probably led to the gradual formation of a 'them' and 'us' situation. This unhealthy state of affairs will probably be aggravated by a lack of concern and urgency on the part of senior managers for increased involvement of the staff in the management of the work organisation. Training and development needs to be introduced at both the operational and top management levels in your organisation.

The low incidence of institutionalised conflict-expressions such as strikes and absenteeism does not necessarily mean that all is well. Indeed this may indicate the possibility of the formation of an informal procedure and of the kind of culture that approves the use of covert unconventional practices in order to remedy the ills of the organisation. Unconventional practices such as pilferage and misuse are already on the menu. However, minor cases of destructive practices should act as warning signs of trouble ahead.

50–74

This score clearly indicates loss of control and the presence of an ineffective work design. Phrases such as 'We still manage' indicates that the management is resorting to *ad hoc* strategies to retain some control. Scapegoating is used to deter others from unconventional practices. This often only makes things worse.

75–100

Scores within this range are a clear sign that your organisation is in hot water. Production-orientated leadership, lack of concern for people, inflexibility and ineffective communication have created a stalement in which trust between managers and staff has either been lost or is in the process of disappearing. Excessive exercise of control and the use of one-way communication ('telling' rather than 'selling') have created a tense and frustrating work environment.

Unconventional practices are no longer uncommon and covert styles are probably preferred to the overt questioning of managerial authority. In effect, unconventional forms of behaviour have been placed on the agenda and an informal agreement for their implementation has been achieved.

The quality of product and services is rapidly deteriorating while management resort to defensive statements such as 'We're busy'. The staff feel that complaining about conditions of employment and work has become pointless. This lack of complaint is often seen as a sign that things are improving, yet to a trained individual it is a clear indication that the organisation is heading for a serious breakdown of work relationships.

All forms of unconventional behaviour can be found; low productivity and inefficiency are the real indicators of their presence. Orders are probably not met on time and the blame is placed on the frequent breakdown of production and service. Covert cases of unconventional behaviour on the part of the staff are no longer intended to attract the attention of the management to the need to establish a more effective communication system and to increase cooperation between the two sides. Indeed, in some situations any hope of sorting out the mess is fading fast. A defiant culture is either being formed or is already well in place. Getting even is probably a recognised way of facilitating and inhibiting work practices.

A complete restructure of work relationships and extensive training are needed if you are concerned for the safety and survival of your organisation.

Questionnaire No. 2
Your Style

This questionnaire is composed of eleven separate sections each containing four statements. For each section you have a total of nine points to distribute amongst the statements that you think are most pertinent to you. You may wish to spread the nine points over several or all of the four statements; alternatively, you may wish to load all nine points on to one single statement. If you really think that only one of the four statements in any section applies to you at all times, and that none of the other three statements is ever true of you, this is fine. However, to achieve a reliable result, we ask you to consider this decision carefully. In your responses, try to be as honest as you possibly can.

1. At work:
a) I would rather do things as part of a group.
b) I like to do things as part of a group, but there are not that many people I can or want to get that close to.
c) I prefer to do things on my own.
d) I do join in with other people, but frankly I prefer my own company.

2. Usually:
a) I am prepared to air my views, but I rarely find that anyone shares them.
b) When it comes to sharing views I like to feel that mine are the same as other people's. If we all think the same, we can't be wrong.
c) I don't like to air my views unless I'm with people who I know share them.
d) I prefer people not to know what I'm thinking, so I will usually say what I think they want to hear.

3. If there's a problem, a good boss:
a) Does not exist. The last thing I or my friends would expect is that a problem would be properly dealt with.
b) Will listen to what I have to say, but won't necessarily do anything about it.
c) Would be hard to find. But I keep that idea to myself. It's everyone for himself in this place.
d) Will always take into account what most people think.

4. In my organisation the normal channels of conflict resolution are:
a) Fair; they're there to benefit everyone.
b) Useless, but that's not an opinion I'd want to share with anyone.
c) Useless, but that's not an opinion I'd share with everyone. Just my friends.
d) Useless, and I don't mind saying so.

5. When it comes to trusting people:
a) I think you can trust some people but not everyone.
b) I'd like to be able to trust people but it's very difficult.
c) I think trust is a two-way thing. Trust them and they trust you.
d) I don't think you can trust anyone, not really deep down.

6. If I'm asked to voice an opinion:
a) I don't usually say what I really think, but what seems to be the best thing to say.
b) I don't mind saying what I think but then I usually agree with what everyone is saying anyway.
c) I don't mind saying what I think but no one ever really seems to agree with me.
d) I won't usually say what I really think, not unless I'm sure the people I'm with agree with me.

7. Rules and regulations:
a) Are all very well but I don't set much store by them and I don't mind who knows it.
b) Are something you should be seen to agree with, and if you don't you should only let your close friends know.
c) Are something you should be seen to agree with, even if you don't believe in them.
d) Are made for the benefit of everyone.

8. At meetings, if there's a point I disagree with:
a) I keep my mouth shut. Not everyone will agree with me.
b) I keep my mouth shut. I don't want anyone to know what I think.
c) I'll say so if I think it is something most people won't be happy about.
d) I'll say so, though most people probably won't agree with me.

9. If I can see that there is a better way of doing my job:
a) I will do it quite openly, but I wouldn't be surprised if I was told not to.
b) I would do it as long as no one except my friends would find out.
c) I would do it as long as no one knew about it. It's better to be seen to go along with things as they are.
d) I will see if other people agree with me.

10. I dislike people who:
a) Pretend to be on your side when they are not.
b) Are open and trusting. The 'hail fellow well met' type.
c) Are sneaky, get into little huddles and keep themselves to themselves.
d) Who think they are the only ones who can have an opinion.

11. If I wanted to get even I:
a) Would do it with other people, but I think it would be best if we kept it to ourselves.
b) Would not involve anyone else and I'd make sure no one knew what I'd done.
c) Would do it with other people and I wouldn't mind other people knowing what we had done.
d) Would not involve anyone else, but I wouldn't mind anyone knowing what I'd done.

SABOTAGE

Now that you have completed the questionnaire, first enter your points in the table provided below and then transfer them to the table on the next page and add them up.

Statement	a	b	c	d
1				
2				
3				
4				
5				
6				
7				
8				
9				
10				
11				

QUESTIONNAIRES

Statement	Lone Ranger	Protester	Sniper	Rebel
1	c	a	d	b
2	a	b	d	c
3	b	d	c	a
4	d	a	b	c
5	b	c	d	a
6	c	b	a	d
7	a	d	c	b
8	d	c	b	a
9	a	d	c	b
10	c	a	b	d
11	d	c	b	a
Total score				

The column with the highest score represents your preferred style of behaviour. An even spread of scores amongst the four columns means that you do not employ any one particular style but that you behave differently at different times. It also means that your behaviour is unpredictable. If the score shows that you do behave in a preferred style, you would be more than likely to take action in that particular style when faced with discontent at work.

Part II

MEANS OF GETTING EVEN

A conveyor belt that appears to have been tampered with; a missing piece of prototype software; pounds of rotten meat products and fish left overnight in an open freezer; the annoying rattling noise made by a handful of washers left in the sealed frame of a new car; the wasted half-ton of fertiliser on the wet factory floor: all these constitute acts of getting even, if we know that they were done deliberately to express resentment against either people or situations in the workplace environment.

In most cases such actions express resentment. Sooner or later, depending on the style and action used, they come to the attention of those against whom the action was taken.

Having examined the four different *styles* in which one can get even, we shall now explore the *actions* that people can take. Our investigations revealed that acts of getting even fall into six categories. These are pilferage, rule-breaking, non-cooperation, destructive practices, disruptive practices and misuse. We shall explore each of these practices in turn and demonstrate how they can be engaged in by individuals or groups, openly or secretly, with varying effects and consequences.

3

PILFERAGE

Lingerie was missing by the caseload. It was literally melting away and no matter what we did, we couldn't stop it from walking out of the warehouse. The women in the packing department knew nothing about it. We even did random security searches, but it all came to nothing. Eventually one day we received a call from one of our catalogue agents saying that he had received someone else's order, a typewriter with four sets of underwear stuffed into one corner of the box.

It turned out that one of our employees, who had set up an agency for selling catalogue stuff, was in collusion with a lad in the packing department. He had been pilfering things, placing them in his girlfriend's order and off they went, transported by our vans to their destination. If the driver hadn't delivered the parcel to the wrong address, we would probably never have known.

Catalogue warehouse manager

Pilferage can cover a wide range of workplace behaviour. Labels such as 'stealing', 'fiddling', 'knock-offs' and 'perks' are commonly applied to this unacceptable but common workplace behaviour. Pilferage here is used to describe:

- The unlawful possession of workplace property for personal use, or
- The provision of unauthorised personnel with such properties.

Employees and pilferage

Of the 176 instances of pilferage which were observed at the research site, Alpha, 96 were perpetrated by the staff. These acts of pilferage can be subdivided as follows:

	Cases
Money	51
Raw materials	38
Production equipment	3
Unauthorised issue of product	3
Product	1
Total	96

The list of items that can be pilfered from organisations is almost inexhaustible. As a manager of a superstore commented. 'When it comes to pilfering nothing is safe around here. Some of it could have really serious consequences. Imagine there is a fire in the store and you reach out for the fire extinguisher and you don't find it there. That happened to us a couple of years back.'

However, as we discovered, the items that people will pilfer can be assigned to a few basic categories. These are, as shown above, money, raw materials, production equipment and products. Another form of pilferage is to provide unauthorised personnel with property belonging to the organisation. The case described at the beginning of this chapter typifies pilferage. A further example is that of a GP whose practice is in an underprivileged area. He regularly provides some patients with medication obtained elsewhere. And again a bar manager in an international hotel described a case where a barmaid who had given in her notice served all the hotel's clients with half-priced drinks one night.

It is commonly assumed that when people pilfer at work, they actually take items out of the workplace. This need not always be the case, however: as there may be a certain amount of danger in attempting to remove bulkier items from the workplace, it may be safer to keep them on the premises. In the hotel, catering and food industries, it is not uncommon for employees to eat or drink their way through the stock. For example, in a large food factory, it was observed that a disgruntled employee who had to work night shifts over the Christmas period was breaking the hot gala pies open, removing the eggs from the centre and then moulding the two pieces back together. On one occasion a message was found inside a pie: *The egg was tasty – Quality Control.*

Another way in which people are able to pilfer without removing the stolen goods from the premises is by giving away food and drinks to other people.

Access

It must be noted that cash, products and other items can only be used as a means of getting even when the staff have access to them: what cannot be got at cannot be pilfered. Most managers are aware of this but at the same time they cannot lock up everything. What is accessible to employees, however, changes from one industry to another and from one organisation to another within the same industry. In most organisations the staff have little or no access to cash. But in organisations which belong to the service sector in general, and the hotel and catering industries in particular, a large proportion of employees are directly involved in monetary transactions with clients on behalf of the organisation. Barmaids, petrol-station attendants, supermarket cashiers and bus and taxi drivers all have easy access to money. This is probably why so many cases of monetary pilferage are reported to have taken place in these industries. The high rate of monetary pilferage amongst the bar staff at Alpha can be explained by the fact that they were frequently involved in serving customers. This direct involvement created many convenient opportunities for them to get even with their employers. Nevertheless, as explained earlier, the sensitive and taboo nature of pilferage meant that it was normally carried out covertly, whether on an individual or group basis.

'It was on the house!'

Doris, a barmaid at the Alpha night-club, approached the Catering Manager and asked him if she could leave work a quarter of an hour earlier so that she could take an earlier bus home. Her request was promptly refused and when she persisted the Manager's reply was, 'Look, it's up to me and I don't feel like letting you go early.'

Disappointed, Doris went back to work but grumbled, 'The top hotels and clubs in town either send their staff home by taxi or give them extra money to get one themselves, except this place. By the time I finish here, I have to get the bus at three in the morning. I won't get home till four and I've got to be up at seven to get the kids ready for school. He's a right bastard. But not to worry. I'll get a taxi and he'll pay for it.'

The next day it was confirmed by Doris herself that she did indeed get a taxi that night and, as she put it, 'It was on the house.'

Doris had used the *Sniper's* style to get even with the manager. As Doris saw it, the only alternative to catching an early bus home was to take a taxi. The fact that the work she did placed her in a position which involved exchanging money for goods with the clients of the organisation provided her with ample opportunities to resolve her discontent – for that night at least. It is worth bearing in mind that access alone does not guarantee success. A good knowledge of the job, working conditions and customers' behaviour, particularly those customers who have regular dealings with the organisation, can be a decisive factor in not getting caught. As she explained later, 'These blokes asked me for a round of drinks. It came to £4.70 and they gave me a fiver and said keep the change. While I was doing the order I pulled a pint of lager for Tony [a regular customer]; he never asks for his receipt. I tilled in the money for the pint and kept the fiver.'

Mobility

The degree to which an individual moves around the workplace, as an essential part of the job, will also help to determine how far and in what way he can get even. Bar staff, waiters, waitresses and door-to-door salespeople all have the advantage of physical mobility – unlike cashiers, computer operators, assembly-line workers and so on. The behaviour of a milkman on his round is not observable to his manager, while a telephone switchboard operator will not be able to move about and may also be under the watchful eye of a supervisor.

The way in which physical mobility could be a definite advantage when it came to getting even was observed at the Alpha. If people behind the bar wanted to 'fiddle', one ploy would be to serve customers as far away from their tills as they possibly could.

At Alpha, the distance between where the money was taken to where the till was situated could make it difficult for either a human observer or for a closed-circuit security camera to check the amount rung up on the till with what was actually served to the customer. As an experienced waitress explained, 'It's not just the distance that makes it easier to fiddle. The further you are from the till the more time you have to have a good look around. You never know who's watching, do you!'

Monetary pilferage

In hotel and catering organisations, periodic stock-checks are often the only means of control. It is extremely difficult, if not impossible, for the management to determine exactly how much of the missing stock is actually lost through monetary pilferage. This is because the loss is calculated as the discrepancy between input (stock) and output measured in terms of the amount of cash generated from the sales of the products or services. Any shortages, therefore, are not necessarily due to the loss of cash. They could equally well be due to the pilferage of raw materials and the unauthorised issue of food and drinks from the bars and kitchens. The inability to pinpoint precisely which activities are responsible for the shortages, the amount and the people involved, is generally described by the managers of such establishments as a headache.

The amounts that were pilfered by employees at Alpha varied from a mere fifty pence to substantial sums of money. Employees, however, did not set out simply to rob the organisation of as much as possible. Certain factors, apart from those connected with access and mobility, determined how much they would take, these included such things as a disagreement with a manager, inconvenience and hardship suffered as a result of management action, a feeling that they had been unjustly treated and so on. It was in relation to these factors that individuals or groups decided how much money would be a fair recompense. The following is a good example of how *Rebels* can act together to pilfer what they believe to be a justified amount of money.

Compensation

At Alpha, as at many similar organisations, the issue of who was responsible for any discrepancies between the total reading on the cash register and the actual amount of cash was a source of constant dispute. It was management policy that every member of staff who dealt with cash should be made responsible for shortages.

One night Jean's till was £5 down and as she had only received £3.50 in tips she was distressed. In her defence she went on to blame the unusually busy night for the mistake which she had made. 'It was so busy I didn't know who to serve. I had an argument with one of my customers. He called me all the names under the sun and after that I couldn't think straight.'

The Catering Manager insisted that she should redress the shortage, otherwise he would simply deduct the money from her pay packet. Jean handed over £3.50 and borrowed another £1.50 from Jane, her workmate. She complained loudly, 'I've worked all night for nothing and not only didn't I make anything, I owe Jane £1.50 . . . it's bloody marvellous!'

During the weekend Jane, who sympathised with Jean, assisted her in 'pinching' £8 from the tills. They said that this would cover the lost tips, with £3 'for compensation'.

The management were ignorant of the compensatory mechanism involved. As far as they were concerned, pilferage was pilferage and a serious crime. Employees were aware of this and knew that if they were caught the least they could expect was summary dismissal. It is therefore not surprising that nearly four out of five acts of pilferage were carried out covertly.

Raw materials

Before embarking on an act of pilferage the individuals involved would give a great deal of consideration to the usefulness of the items to be taken. After money, raw materials (such as bottles of drink) were the second choice, though pilferage of other things such as products (in prepared or semi-prepared forms), production and non-production equipment was not uncommon, especially with those individuals who had little access to cash.

Caught red-handed

A cleaner was caught red-handed rummaging around in the stationery cupboard by the office staff. She admitted that she was looking for A4 paper which she could use in a typewriter she had obtained from her previous employment. In her defence she maintained that she was simply unable to afford good-quality typing paper.

Where pilferage of food and drink was concerned, a collective action would often be preferred as being the most effective.

Mixing pleasure with business

Three bar staff were asked to work on their night off because a large party (over 450 guests) had been booked at the last minute. However, they did this reluctantly and decided to get even with the manager by mixing pleasure with business.

Every now and then when one of them served a customer, a deliberate mistake was made and the drink was left on the shelf. The second person would remove the drink from the top shelf and place it on the sink underneath the bar. The third person, who would be replacing washed glasses on the bottom shelves, would then have the drink which had been left under the bar. This was repeated at least three times for each of them. Each time they drank to someone they knew: the first toast was to their colleagues, another was to the management, and there was even one to Elton John.

When it came to removing items from the workplace, Rebel action was preferred to the Sniper's approach because it was felt that there was safety in numbers. Moreover, it was believed that only organised group action would provide the necessary manpower to obtain and hide the pilfered items and remove them from the workplace, as in the following instance.

New glasses

New glasses were issued to the bars. The small glasses were packed in boxes of six. Two barmaids and a barman were reported to have taken six boxes for themselves and to have hidden them underneath the bar until Saturday night. At the end of that Saturday shift, the two barmaids each secreted three boxes of glasses in their capacious handbags. Once outside the club, they each gave one box to the barman.

Pilferage was thus often resorted to as a means of getting even with employers. As a reaction to management policies and practices it is too well known to be denied by management. Nevertheless its occurrence is often not publicly acknowledged, because it implies that managers are not able to control their staff.

Management and pilferage

Managers themselves are employees in the eyes of their superiors. They too can be tempted to pilfer in order to get even and, like staff, they have a preference for money. At Alpha alone, more than half of the 80 cases of pilferage which involved management were of a monetary nature. These acts of pilferage were carried out by the general and box-office managers, catering managers and their assistants. It was the catering managers, however, who were responsible for the majority of instances. This is not unusual. As with staff, the things that managers can pilfer will depend on what they have access to. Catering managers, as part of their job, generally have easier access to money that their colleagues, though naturally all managers should have easier access than their employees to any item.

Acts of pilferage on the part of managers at Alpha can be subdivided as follows:

	Cases
Money	46
Unauthorised issue of product	24
Product	7
Raw materials	3
Total	80

The managers did not like to pilfer products and raw materials because the catering and general managers in particular were responsible for the loss of raw materials from their respective departments. However, the money generated by the catering side came from different units, such as several cash registers in different bars, the restaurant and the cloakroom. On the general side the main source of income was the admission money, which was kept in one till in the box-office. As a rule the catering side of the organisation generated much more income than the general side, and this constituted an informal measure of the catering manager's relative status. It was also a potential source of discontent and rendered the catering managers vulnerable to acts of getting even on the part of the general manager. The fact that the catering manager formally held a lower position than the general manager placed him or her in an unenviable position. In short, the general manager enjoyed prerogatives that were not shared by the box-office and catering managers and their assistants.

Catering managers who did not or could not form good relationships with the general manager could become the target of acts of getting even. Within the hotel and catering industry, it is generally understood that the general manager should be 'looked after' by the catering manager. As one experienced catering manager put it, 'It's more than just a peace offering, it's insurance you need to take out against the loss of all your stock – accidents *could* happen.'

At the end of a busy Friday night, one such accident did occur at Alpha.

The cash bags

Rod, the Catering Manager, following normal procedure asked one of the glass-collectors to take the cash bags containing the bar takings upstairs to the main office. There the General Manager told the glass-collector to leave them and return to his duties. The following day it was announced that a cash bag containing £300 was 'missing'. A reliable source said, 'It's near Christmas and the big boss needs to pay his expenses. The poor new Catering Manager has had to learn the hard way. I bet he was asked to do something and refused. It's not the first time a cash bag has gone missing anyway.'

General managers could and would use Sniper tactics when pilfering.

Assistant managers would also use Sniper tactics but the amount of money pilfered by them was never as much as that which was taken by the catering or general managers. The most important reason for this was their relative lack of access to money and, to a lesser degree, their lack of authority. Cases of pilferage on the part of the assistants were referred to by their immediate superiors as 'nothing more than a quid here and there'. For example, the money which was received for the purchase of champagne or a vintage bottle of wine would sometimes be appropriated by the assistants instead of being put through the till. As one explained, 'It's only when it's really busy and when no one's watching that it's possible to pull that one off. If the boss sees you, you've had it. The least that's likely to happen is that you won't get a good report and never

59

become a manager of your own place. Besides that, you can't go really mad and take lots of money because that would show up badly on the books.'

The assistant general manager was mainly responsible for repair and maintenance, though one discontented assistant said he sometimes felt no better than a glorified bouncer. The occupant of this position in the organisation had even less access to money than did the assistant catering manager, but access to money could be engineered.

Assistant general manager

'One night I was really pissed off! Up to here with it! The boss had a right go at me and it wasn't even my fault. Anyhow, I said to myself, "That's done it." After one in the morning when the box-office was closed I told Bobby, the door supervisor, to take a walk. Then I let in about twenty guys, right up to two o'clock. Three quid each, straight into my pocket. They were really pleased about it, because they knew they couldn't get in anywhere else at that time of night. The money wasn't much but I felt better.'

In the same way that employees used pilferage as a means of expressing their discontent with management, managers also used acts of pilferage as a means of showing dis-agreement with *their* superiors. In these instances the Rebel approach was not uncommon. This was largely because it was company policy to hold the management of a branch responsible as a group for anything that went wrong: 'Whenever something goes wrong . . . we all get a bollocking from the directors.'

This meant that at such times the directors had unintentio-nally created a hesitant mutuality amongst the branch's man-agers. As they had all been reprimanded or penalised – losing out on their bonuses, for example – they would react against this and behave as a group of Rebels. They could not expect those who formed a much larger group within the organisation, the staff, to share their views. Their power, authority and access meant that when the managers did get together they could 'pull off a big one', as illustrated by the following case.

Sharing the loot

One Sunday night, a 'Northern Soul' party was booked at Alpha's sister branch. Some new bar staff were taken on and were told by the Catering Manager to put a glass in their till drawers so that they could not be closed. At the end of the night the £960 from these four tills were handed over to the Catering Manager. A reliable source revealed that after closing time two new till rolls were made up in the office for the amount of £360 and the rest was split between the Catering and General Managers.

Having bogus employees on the books was another way in which managers could pilfer money. In large organisations, with a large staff turnover, it is difficult to keep track of who has left and when. A retired general manager of a branch in London explained how he would operate this 'fiddle': 'Often we'd get foreign students in their last year, who intend to go back home. Once they left you'd bring them back on the books for a while for a month or so. The cashiers who do the wages would never see the applicants anyway. All they would be interested in was the National Insurance number and an address.'

Managers did not particularly like to pilfer service and production equipment as they displayed a proprietorial attitude towards the organisation and its equipment. As they seemed to regard the place as their own, they did not like to see the service and production equipment impaired in any way. On the other hand, this attitude made them vulnerable to being 'got at' by resentful employees. One catering manager explained, 'Any piece of equipment which goes missing from here needs to be replaced. To do that the General Manager has to either pay for it from here or invoice it through Head Office. Then the trouble starts. Besides, it doesn't look good when things go missing and when it comes to the annual bonuses, we lose out.'

Motives and meanings

Table 1

	Managers' motives				Employees' motives			
Pilferage	P	I	E	T	P	I	E	T
1. Raw materials	0	3	0	3	6	28	4	38
2. Money	36	9	1	46	16	30	5	51
3. Product	0	7	0	7	1	0	0	1
4. Pro-equipment	0	0	0	0	1	2	0	3
5. Giving away	3	21	0	24	2	1	0	3
Total	39	40	1	80	26	61	9	96

P=Personal   I=Internal   E=External   T=Total

At Alpha the managers' motives were almost equally divided between internal (40) and personal types (39). Only one case had an external motive.

The staff's major source of discontent lay within the organisation (61 cases). Less than a third of the cases (26) were ascribable to personal motives, and approximately one-fifth (9) to external motives.

It may seem inevitable that more acts of pilferage on the part of the staff were due to internal motives than was the case with the managers; but we must also note that the difference was not as great as one might expect. We can deduce from this that the managers at Alpha are perhaps not *that* much happier than their employees.

Indeed, the meaning ascribed to their actions by both staff and managers implied that they felt their contribution to be undervalued by those above them. Both managers and staff felt that they were worth a lot more than they were paid. The staff blamed the managers for their being under-remunerated while the managers in turn blamed *their* superiors. Whenever possible both staff and managers would attempt to correct the imbalance. For example, when the representatives of a brewery gave the club dozens of crates of drinks for the staff on a night when they were holding a promotion party, the managers sold the bottles to the customers and kept the money for themselves. The General Manager said, 'What we have to do on these nights is more than we get paid for, so it's only fair to keep some to ourselves.'

Apart from a feeling of being undervalued and underpaid, the other major motives attributed by staff to their actions were frustration, necessity, challenging authority and the desire to exercise a certain degree of control over their work. Some of the cases observed earlier in the chapter – Doris pilfering money for her taxi fare; Jean and Jane pilfering money to make up for the mistake on the till and the bar staff consuming alcohol when asked to work an extra night – were motivated by feelings of frustration originating from work relationships within the organisation. The cleaner who attempted to steal typing paper from the office did so out of necessity and the bar staff who took home boxes of glasses did so because they felt their wages were too low to enable them to purchase their own.

However, the managers' motives were mainly both internal and personal. Financial gain was the main motive for monetary pilferage, and the need for recognition, status and autonomy were the main reasons for the unauthorised issue of products and raw materials. In all the cases described above concerning the managers the main motivation was financial gain.

From Table 1 one can see that the two main types of item pilfered by staff were money and raw materials. It was the usefulness of items that determined whether or not they were worth stealing. Money and raw materials were regarded as the most useful, followed in descending order by products and production and non-production equipment.

The managers also pilfered mostly money or raw materials; but unlike the staff they also had a tendency to give away free drinks and food. As a rule the staff did not like to use this form of pilfering, because they feared the consequences of discovery. Moreover, the power to enforce payment to some extent satisfied their desire for autonomy and control over their work. A customer who refused to pay allowed a bar worker to bring into play some very powerful elements – the managers and doormen.

In contrast the managers used *their* power to give people free drinks and meals as a means of gaining recognition. It must be noted that company regulations forbade the use of the night-club and its facilities for the entertainment of personal guests. When a manager had personal guests it obviously allowed him to exercise authority and control through playing the role of 'mine host' with the organisation's stock. The impression he would give was not just that he owned the 'things' but also the people who fetched and carried those things.

Finally, while more individual acts of pilferage were carried out by staff than by managers, it was the managers who, because of their easier access to money and so on, took the lion's share of the loot.

Styles

Table 2

Pilferage	Lone Ranger	Sniper	Protester	Rebel	Total
Manager	30	1	42	7	80
Employee	10	29	7	50	96

The style chosen by an individual to carry out an act of pilferage is closely related to his position in the organisation. As Table 2 shows, at Alpha the staff chose mainly the covert styles of the Rebel or Sniper while the managers adopted mainly the open styles of the Protester or Lone Ranger, even though, as illustrated by the cases in the main body of this chapter, they would also employ Sniper or Rebel style if the action merited this approach.

The fact that the staff's actions were mainly covert and the managers' overt is significant. It demonstrates that while the act of pilferage itself is regarded seriously and can have severe repercussions, an individual's fear of discovery is obviously tempered by other factors. If the individual is a member of staff he generally has less power and authority and is under the watchful eyes of his superiors. Hence if he acts openly the likelihood of being caught red-handed is quite high. A manager, on the other hand, has more power and authority and does not have his superiors constantly in evidence. It was interesting to observe, however, that when Alpha was honoured with a visit from the higher echelons of the organisation the managers would then behave with the greatest propriety and display an impressive regard for the rules of the organisation.

The power and authority wielded by managers over their subordinates also meant that the managers were not overly concerned about being reported to Head Office. One evening Glen, a catering manager, was standing at the bar with some of his friends. They were imbibing alcoholic beverages 'on the house' when one of his friends questioned the wisdom of standing there and openly drinking 'free booze' in front of the staff. 'It's not on really, is it?'

Glen, who had become more expansive as the night wore on, took another mouthful of his free drink and said, 'Well look, I'm not a bad manager. I turn a blind eye to a lot of things and I expect them to do the same. They know which side their bread's buttered on. But if anyone did do the dirty on me and I lost my job I'd be taking a few people with me.'

The managers also believed that the staff's lack of loyalty to the organisation was a further protection against being reported to Head Office, so that the staff would not 'grass' whatever they observe the managers doing: 'They hate this place so much, they're not going to waste time reporting us for pinching here and there. They're doing it themselves all the time anyway.'

The staff, however, could not expect the same leniency from the managers. The managers were under constant pressure from Head Office to put an end to pilfering. It was therefore predictable that now and then a scapegoat would be found to carry the blame for the losses which the club suffered. Each individual member of staff, therefore, had to be constantly vigilant to avoid being the one on whom all the blame could be heaped.

Summary

Pilferage is an act of stealing which is carried out by both manager and employees. The items which will be pilfered will be determined by an individual's access to them, the degree to which he is mobile within the workplace and the usefulness of the items which can be pilfered. Money is deemed as the most useful item which can be pilfered. Items do not have to be removed from the workplace in order to be pilfered. Managers and employees can consume food and drink or give away food and drink to customers and colleagues. The motives for pilferage were largely attributed to circumstances within the organisation: difficult work relationships, a feeling of being undervalued or frustration.

Pilferage is an act of defiance which can have serious repercussions for the perpetrator if his identity is discovered. However, while employees would generally carry out acts of pilferage covertly, the managers, in the absence of *their* superiors, would at times pilfer money and other items quite openly. Even so, managers and employees felt that there was safety in numbers and would mainly operate in groups, the managers as Protesters and the staff as Rebels.

4

RULE-BREAKING

An entire city and the surrounding villages had to be evacuated. Hundreds of families became homeless and the lives and health of the old, the young and the unborn were affected. Herds of cattle and other livestock had to be destroyed. Millions of roubles'-worth of damage had been done, and three years later the farmers in Norway were still unable to sell their reindeer meat. All of this is because three operators in the USSR's Chernobyl nuclear power station had unilaterally decided to ignore the rules and regulations concerning safety.

Rule-breaking is not an uncommon practice. We have all heard the expression, 'Rules are made to be broken', and we have all seen examples of this in our own work environments. Some studies have indicated that in some organisations rule-breaking has even become institutionalised. Others have demonstrated that without some form of rule-breaking the performance of normal daily operations would be seriously impaired. In a medium-sized plant belonging to a well-known food factory, it was observed that one of the regulations, specifying the wearing of special but awkwardly designed hats in order to avoid contamination of the food, was repeatedly broken. As one supervisor explained. 'Here, everybody's got their hats in their pockets, ready in case a factory inspector turns up. If we did everything by the book, we'd have to close this place right away.'

We observed that in many cases rule-breaking was employed as a deliberate attempt to get even. The term 'rule-breaking' is used to describe those situations where specific rules and regulations advocated by the organisation or other related agencies regarding a particular function or task, work relationship, or working environment, are deliberately ignored in order to express resentment against those who are either directly or indirectly involved in creating these rules and regulations and/or in their enforcement within the work environment.

At Alpha, rule-breaking accounted for the second highest number of cases of getting even. Of the 98 cases observed, the staff were responsible for more than two-thirds (71 cases) and the managers for the remaining 27 cases.

Table 3

Rule-Breaking

	Management	Employees	Total
Working conditions	16	40	56
Production time	8	14	22
Raw materials	0	10	10
Service	0	5	5
Product	1	1	2
Selling damaged goods	1	1	2
Working hours	1	0	1
Total	27	71	98

It was interesting that in nearly half of the cases it was the rules and regulations concerning the suitability of working conditions that were broken. The other sub-categories shown in Table 3 concerned production, provision of service, use of raw materials, the standard of service or products, and working hours.

Staff and rule-breaking

In most hotel and catering organisations, and others in the service sector, the management reserve the right to modify, alter and add to the existing regulations as and when they see fit. Employees, however, in turn modify, alter and break these rules to get even with their employers. Indeed, at Alpha this process of rule-breaking was found to be in operation at almost all levels of the hierarchy.

As in many organisations of its kind, at Alpha the contents of the bars were protected by steel shutters when the bars are not in use. The bar staff were frequently reminded by the management that it was important to ensure that the shutters were securely fastened before they left the bar. At Alpha the shutters were of the pull-down type, which had the advantage of being out of sight when not in use.

For about six months the bar staff continually made complaints about shutters on the main bar. Often one or more of the steel shutters would not come down until a great deal of energy and effort had been expended. This process sometimes added as much as twenty-five minutes to the staff's closing operations. The management, however, consistently ignored the fact that it was their responsibility to maintain them in good working order. The General Manager often said that the cost of repairing or replacing them would be astronomical. This unsatisfactory state of affairs continued until one night a shutter unexpectedly slammed down of its own accord, frightening everyone in its vicinity. Joanne, a barmaid, was the only person who actually saw what happened. She was serving 'two drunk Paddies' who were standing almost beneath the shutter. She was walking back to them with two pints of Guinness when she heard a strange noise. She looked up just in time to see the shutter falling down. One of the two men, who had his back to the bar, got such a fright that he dived under the nearest table just as the shutter hit the bar top. He was shaking as he was helped out from under the table.

This incident finally impressed on the management that it was time to install new shutters. Typically, new rules for their daily operation and maintenance were also introduced by the General Manager. A special meeting was called to announce these new rules and regulations. 'These shutters cost a thousand quid. More than you lot are worth. I can replace the lot of you any time I want, but I can't afford those shutters again. Make sure that they're not dropped on to the counter, or else.'

The view that the rules concerning the shutters should be ignored soon became a shared one. The staff behind that bar were particularly aggrieved that the management regarded them as less valuable than the shutters. As one employee pointed out. 'If the shutters are worth more than us, it makes you wonder just how much we're each worth . . . Down with those shutters!'

In this case the bar staff came together to form a group of Rebels. The very people who had called for the replacement of the old shutters were now covertly pulling down the new shutters so vigorously that they were soon rendered useless. As the bar staff had continually complained about the old shutters for months, the managers did not believe that they could be responsible for the state of the new shutters and blamed bad workmanship.

This case is typical of the kind where the underlying philosophy of a new rule will ultimately become the very reason for it to be broken.

The rule of 'first come, first served' was one which was particularly liable to be broken. This was mainly because the bar staff would always endeavour to serve, as soon as they possibly could, those whom they knew would tip. Sheila explained why, during the Christmas period, she would serve her 'regulars' more promptly than others: 'The point is that with the wages that we get, we can't afford to do as we're told. They don't pay us enough, so why should we do what they say? I've got to get money for the kids' clothes somehow. I make sure that I do my job but in the way I like it. After all, I'm not a slave.'

The customers who expected prompt service and did not mind paying for it were observed to reinforce this behaviour. Some believed that 'One way of being looked after by the staff during the Christmas period is to get them on your side by tipping during November and December.'

Customers who regularly tip the bar staff can be seen as 'second paymasters'. This is not unique to Alpha: in casinos croupiers can receive as much as twenty or thirty times their normal salary in the form of gratuities. The bar staff would attempt to let the non-tippers know by various means that tipping was the path to prompt and cheerful service – for example, by effusively thanking those who did tip or by displaying great care that the tippers' orders were just as they wanted them, with exactly the right amount of ice and lemonade.

Those customers who failed to learn that tipping would lead to prompt service would often have to wait for half an hour before being served. Customers who responded to the staff's effective programme of 'behaviour modification' came to be known as 'regulars'. If in time a customer was labelled as 'all right' this meant that he did not care whether or not he received a receipt with his change. This, of course, meant that the bar staff could (if they wished to do so and the time was right) pilfer the money for that round of drinks.

Managers and rule-breaking

On the whole, when managers resorted to rule-breaking more people were affected by their actions than when employees did so. It should also be noted that when managers broke the rules this did not always constitute an act of getting even. Sometimes the managers received instructions from Head Office that required them to break the rules, but their actions would be viewed by their employees as deliberate attempts to make working life harder for them. During one particularly cold winter the management received a directive from Head Office requiring them to reduce overhead costs. In response to this, and despite the fact that it was bitterly cold, the heating was turned down and the managers spent as much time as possible warmly ensconced in their heated offices, leaving their employees to brave the Arctic conditions of the night-club. At weekends as the club filled up with customers it would naturally become warmer, but during the week business would often be slack for the first three hours of the evening, only becoming busy when the public houses emptied.

On one very cold night, despite the staff's pleas that the club should be at least as warm as specified by the Health and Safety Regulations, the management refused to turn up the heating. A bar supervisor was told that the staff were feeling so cold because they were not working hard enough. The General Manager's comment worked its way along the grapevine and eventually reached Deliah, who was infuriated and said to her three fellow bar staff, 'They don't care about us standing here like dummies in short sleeves, while they're wearing suits.'

She went on to suggest that drinking brandy would be a good means of keeping warm: 'I've seen it on the telly. When people get caught in the snow, brandy does them good.' The four of them soon felt more sanguine.

Occasionally the managers' breach of a particular rule was only meant to affect the clients but the employees would also be affected. One sultry summer evening the air-conditioning and extractors were switched off. A disgruntled assistant catering manager who suffered from mild bronchitis could not refrain from complaining to the staff: 'That's the General Manager for you. It's all right for him to sit in his office with the windows open and the fan going. What about us? [Pausing to cough.] He says when the place is hot the customers drink more. My boss [the Catering Manager] told him that this place is supposed to be a club not a bloody oven, but he said that you've got to break the rules if you want to show a profit. What a bastard!'

Where managers used their unilateral right to make a new rule that was interpreted by the staff as 'getting at them', the employees would show their resentment by simply ignoring the new rule.

The directors come over

The General Manager called for an emergency meeting and explained: 'Some of you probably know that last week the directors came over. I was really embarrassed – staff were taking breaks as if it was a holiday camp. I know it was breaktime but directors don't like to see you lot sitting around and rightly so. It doesn't make us managers look good. It makes them wonder what sort of outfit we're running here. So from today, you can have twenty minutes' break for every four hours you work and you take that break at the beginning of the session. That's the rule from now on. Right?'

The employees' response to the new rule was to attempt to get even in various ways. Some, like Ellen, adopted Sniper tactics. She would dispose of the change in her till as quickly as possible and then wander around the club at the busiest time. If asked what she was doing Ellen would be ready with the excuse that she was looking for the Catering Manager to ask for some change.

Others adopted Rebel tactics. A group of bar staff made arrangements to meet regularly in the powder room at approximately 11.45 p.m. when their presence behind the bars would be most required. Here they could not be seen by the Catering Manager and could socialise and smoke cigarettes.

Another Rebel group, the staff on another bar, decided that they should each have a drink and a quarter of an hour downstairs in the cloakroom. Helena, the cloakroom attendant, was to be supplied with rum and blacks for harbouring the absentee workers.

It was much easier for the managers to shirk their responsibilities during working hours. They would simply leave the club or retire to the office. In these situations staff were told by the managers' assistants that they had 'popped out on business'. In fact the managers of the three local IEC night-clubs would visit each other's clubs, ostensibly on business, but in reality to avail themselves of the amenities or merely to escape, however briefly, from their own workplace.

Raw materials

For managers who work in the hotel and catering and other service industries, 'stock' becomes more than just a word to describe what is on the shelves or in the store-rooms. It has become a measure by which their superiors can calculate their managerial worth. The smaller the discrepancy between the stock-sheets and the stock-checks, the more highly will the manager be thought of by his superiors. At Alpha, managers sometimes resorted to rule-breaking to compensate for missing stock. This was material that had been pilfered, wasted or destroyed but not reported. For example, the management occasionally stipulated that only one measure of lemonade or Coke should be provided with spirits, rather than the generous amounts that were normally given. This strategy was usually employed by the managers when the stock was in a desperate state. Not a great deal of money could be saved by restricting the amounts of lemonade and Coke given with the spirits. However, each time that the management imposed this rule the staff knew that 'The stocks are down and the Catering Manager's in trouble' (Brian).

The staff would then use this as an opportunity to get even by giving even more generous amounts of lemonade and Coke than was the norm. At other times, however, this was not done to get even but to avoid arguments with intoxicated and at times violent clients. As Fiona explained, 'One Wednesday

74

night when I served one bloke and gave him just as much lemonade as the manager said, he went berserk, swearing and threatening me. He said, "I'm paying bloody good money for that drink, fill it up . . . you robbing swine." So I said to myself to hell with the stock, never mind the damn measures, it's not worth the bother.'

Rule-breaking: Meanings and motives

Table 4

Areas of Rule-breaking	Managers' motives				Employees' motives			
	P	I	E	T	P	I	E	T
1 Service	0	0	0	0	2	3	0	5
2 Working hours	1	0	0	1	0	0	0	0
3 Working conditions	12	4	0	16	8	8	24	40
4 Raw material	0	0	0	0	0	4	6	10
5 Production time	2	6	0	8	0	14	0	14
6 Product	0	1	0	1	0	1	0	1
7 Selling damaged goods	0	1	0	1	0	1	0	1
Total	15	12	0	27	10	31	30	71

P=Personal   I=Internal   E=External   T=Total

In Table 4, of the 27 cases recorded on the part of the managers more than half had personal reasons and 12 had motives attributable to the work environment. In these latter cases the desire for more control over the staff and their activities, autonomy and profit maximisation were the main reasons for attempting to get even.

These motives for rule-breaking need to be considered in relation to sources of disagreement which may lie outside the work environment, yet still influence the work relations of the managers with their employees. For the managers of Alpha, working for IEC had its undesirable aspects too. They had to manage the activities of their employees and the branch as a whole within the confines of the rules and regulations issued by Head Office, who expected them to be complied with throughout the company. These rules and regulations were amended and changed periodically. Such a body of procedural and normative rules, however, did not take into account the individual characteristics of each branch, the task in hand, the nature of operations and the location of the organisation. Not surprisingly, the managers either regarded the existing rules as inadequate, which meant that there was a need for new rule-making on their part, or they felt frustrated and constrained by rules that often denied them their right as managers to exercise autonomy in 'their' organisation.

Of the 71 staff cases recorded, 31 had internal motives, 10 had personal motives and 30 had motives which stemmed from outside the working environment. Exercising autonomy, revenge, challenging authority and the desire to facilitate the work process, were amongst the main motives for the staff's actions.

In the above cases concerning the shutter and that of Deliah and her workmates who drank brandy to keep warm, the staff were motivated by the desire for revenge. Ellen's walkabout and the congregating of staff in the powder-room were challenges to management's authority.

Most cases of rule-breaking on the part of the staff were in response to managers' actions. The regulations concerning working conditions, production time and service and the use of raw materials were the main sources of discontent.

At times the discontent fostered by work relationships with employers was expressed in terms of rule-breaking simply because the employees felt powerless to change the rules restricting their activities and the control that was exercised over their jobs: it was a last resort.

The staff would also break the rules when they were suspicious of the intention behind them. For example, one night the Catering Manager told the bar staff to use two particular beer pumps. The staff, as they put it, 'knew something wasn't right'. It was discovered later that these pumps contained 80 gallons of beer that had already been written off by the brewery. The managers intended to sell these 80 gallons to redress some of the imbalances that customarily appeared on the stock-checks.

Not only were the staff reluctant to serve the customers with that brand of beer, but they also explained to the customers that the beer was unfit for consumption.

The managers would ignore the kind of rule-breaking which facilitated work processes or made savings on raw materials and production time. In fact minor rule-breaking of any kind was normally tolerated by the managers. However, if a manager wished to exert his authority he could punish a member of staff for rule-breaking when he would not normally do so.

However, when minor rule-breaking, such as serving two customers at once to save time and increase tips, was suddenly questioned by the management, the staff would then retaliate by 'working to rule'. This would mean that it would take them longer to serve the customers and the managers would then receive many complaints about the slow service. If rule-breaking seems to be a simple strategy to get even, the meanings and motives behind it are not always so straightforward.

Styles

Table 5

Rule-breaking style:	Lone Ranger	Sniper	Protester	Rebel	Total
Managers	7	16	4	0	27
Employees	7	41	9	14	71

Both managers and staff showed a preference for Sniper tactics when it came to rule-breaking. Of the cases described in this chapter, that of Ellen was a Sniper action; the cases concerning the shutters, Deliah and the brandy, and the impromptu meetings in the powder-room were all Rebel actions. The case where the managers attempted to sell suspect beer was that of Protesters' action. The following is a case of Sniper action on the part of the management.

After investigating a claim by a regular customer who, as he put it, 'knew his ale', that what he was being served tasted like water, it was discovered that Bill the Catering Manager was compensating for the predictable monthly loss of stock by adding water to the beer tanks through the view-hole located on the top of the otherwise sealed tanks.

Sniper tactics were often employed in cases when the breaking of certain rules could be punishable by summary dismissal or prosecution. As the Floor Manager of a small neighbouring night-club explained, 'Diluting beer, tampering with the measures and allowing under-aged youngsters to be served with alcohol isn't new. It's been done before but you never hear about it. It's a case of doing it and forgetting about it. Can you imagine getting sacked on those charges . . . you could kiss goodbye to your career and that's the truth.'

Employees also chose to adopt Sniper action when their acts of rule-breaking, if discovered, could have had serious consequences. In a monthly meeting the General Manager warned: 'I shouldn't have to remind you that buying, selling and trading when you are supposed to be working is an act of indiscipline. It's in the IEC rule book and you know it. However, it seems that there are one or two of you who don't realise that selling knocked-off property is illegal and if they're caught here not only will they get the sack straight away, they will probably be prosecuted for possessing stolen goods. So pack it in! The security have been instructed to be particularly vigilant about this . . . it's bad for you and the company's reputation is at risk.'

The warning, however, did not deter Brenda from occasionally bringing to work items which she would sell for a fifth of the retail price.

However, like any other group of people the staff at Alpha could break a rule collectively and openly, in the style of the Protester, if they felt strongly enough about the issue involved. Examples of such situations have been given above but here is a particularly memorable case.

Aerobic dancing

During the late seventies aerobic dancing was becoming more and more popular and IEC decided to exploit this new fashion. The staff of 16 IEC night-clubs were given jogging pants and T-shirts, and were told to adopt a 'friendly style' and dance to the music at the same time as serving the customers. Alpha's managers believed this to be a potentially highly profitable venture and asked Regional Headquarters if they could also exploit this new fashion. The staff, on the other hand, did not take to this new idea at all. Some saw it as demeaning; 'There's no way I'm going to stand here like a bloody fool, wiggling my bottom. And have you seen the cut of these uniforms? They make us look like God knows what. They're too tight in the wrong places and they make the men look as if they're just out of Alcatraz. There's absolutely no way I can stomach doing this dancing and serving business. I'm employed as a barmaid not a dancer. They'll be expecting us to go topless next. No way am I going to do it.' And this was from Marianne, who was normally a reticent, quietly spoken person.

Some members of the staff did not see it in quite this way. In other circumstances they thought the new gimmick might be fun, but they felt that they were being exploited in order to make Alpha a more profitable organisation, and this they found galling in the extreme. There was much anger and resentment generated against the managers by the aerobic dancing proposal. All the female staff refused to wear the new uniforms and to dance behind the bar. When threatened with instant dismissal by the General Manager, Hilda reminded them that IEC would not want the bad publicity which would be caused by 22 of the staff taking them to the Industrial Tribunal for unfair dismissal. The managers had no option but to discard the project.

Summary

The rules and regulations concerning working conditions are the most susceptible to being broken. Bar staff will frequently break the 'first come first served' rule in order to obtain as many gratuities as possible. When managers break rules many more people can be affected by their actions than when employees fail to observe the regulations.

While managers often have to institute new rules as a result of a directive from Head Office, whether or not they agree with the rules, their staff are often unaware that managers are not acting on their own initiative. Employees can therefore interpret the introduction of new rules by managers as a deliberate action *against* the staff. In turn the employees will deliberately ignore or break the new rule. Ineffective channels of communication can be seen as directly responsible for employees regarding new rules as a strategy on the part of managers to render their working life more difficult.

Motives for rule-breaking by managers were almost equally personal and internal, while internal and external motives predominated for employees.

Both managers and employees preferred Sniper tactics in breaking organisational rules and regulations.

5

DESTRUCTIVE PRACTICES

When fire engulfed a Hollywood studios, millions of dollars'-worth of damage had been done before it could be brought under control. It was suspected that a company security officer was responsible and he was arrested on a charge of arson.

The most controversial acts of getting even that were observed were those that involved wilfully destroying and damaging the work environment.

Destructive practices can be separated into three distinct categories of behaviour – destruction, inaction and wastage.

Destruction

Table 6

Items	Employees	Managers	Total
Raw materials	9	0	9
Production equipment	40	0	40
Product	1	0	1
Non-production equipment	4	0	4
Total	54	0	54

As Table 6 shows, it was only the staff who attempted to get even by destroying or damaging the work environment. The managers were reluctant to resort to this kind of action for a variety of reasons, the main one being that they were held responsible for the cost of damages. It could be argued that the policy of rendering managers accountable for damages was successful in that it prevented the managers from adopting this kind of action.

Management's reluctance to employ destructive practices was also due to the fact that they were aware of the consequences that would follow if they were caught. They knew that this was regarded as despicable and criminal by the organisation and by society as a whole. To have a report of having carried out a destructive action in their file would have ruined their chances of starting new careers elsewhere.

Furthermore, unlike the staff, the managers also had a proprietorial attitude to the organisation and 'the things which were in it'. They would talk of 'my tills', 'my pumps', 'my stock', 'my staff'. Thus when the employees wanted to get even with the managers, destruction presented itself as a particularly effective means.

Kitchen on fire

It was known that the relationship between Roberto the chef and the Catering Manager was not an amicable one and that Roberto was waiting for an opportunity to 'get at' him. One Friday evening the management were told that a group of directors were coming to inspect the club at ten that night. This was an unexpected turn of events and the managers immediately began to ensure that everything in the club was as it should be. The Catering Manager informed the staff – including the chef – that it was important that everything should be shipshape when the visitation took place.

Around 9 p.m. an argument between the chef and the Catering Manager ensued. Some of the employees raised their eyes heavenwards and asked, 'What's Roberto cooking up now?'

At 9.30 p.m. Roberto's excited Italian voice drew the staff of the nearby bar to the kitchen, '*Mama mia*! My kitchen she is burning! Help . . . help!'

Inside the smoke-filled kitchen, Roberto in his once white uniform, was enthusiastically tackling a fire in one of the fryers with a blanket and a powder extinguisher. The Catering Manager had to get on his hands and knees to ensure that the kitchen was ready for inspection.

Some time later Roberto explained: 'The best way to get at the Catering Manager is to get at his kitchen. That gets him really worried.'

The staff at Alpha preferred to destroy production equipment (40 out of 54 cases) rather than non-production equipment or raw materials because it was the most direct way of interfering with the processes of production and service and hence the most effective way of getting at the managers. The most popular pieces of production equipment to be destroyed were drinking-glasses and pint mugs. As much as £400-worth of glasses could be destroyed in a month. The bar staff could relieve their feelings by deliberately smashing the glasses on the floor, but this was generally held to be a rather impractical and potentially dangerous activity. Simply throwing the glasses away was found to be the best and most efficient method. In this way not only were they getting at what they saw as the managers' property, but they were putting 'a spanner in the works' as well.

Broken glass

Luke, a student by day and a barman at the weekends, confided: 'One night I was completely fed up. You know I only get a partial grant and I don't like to ask my dad to cough up. It would make quite a hole in his salary, so I work in this dump to make it up! I could do with this weekend to revise for my exams, but I can't afford to lose my wages and any money we can nick. Well, I brought in my notes to look at when it's quiet and now just as I could do with being left alone the Catering

Manager comes along and starts picking on me. He says I look sloppy, I'm not wearing this gear properly and then he says, when did I last wash my hair? Typical bourgeois stupid management remark to make, just because my hair's down to my shoulders. So I'm fed up and I 'accidentally' drop several pint mugs on to the floor at the end of the bar. I'm leaning on the bar and my elbow 'slips' and knocks them off.

'Nobody's there, right? I don't want to hurt anyone, but then I realise what I've done. Now I've got to clear the mess up, right? A berk, that's what I am. So I clear it up and now I'm in a worse mood than ever, so I decided I'm not washing any more than I have to anyway that night, so when I can, when Maggie's not looking I just drop them in the bin. And of course now I'm doing it, I notice that's what other people are doing. And you know Tina? She absolutely detests washing ashtrays. Well, when Maggie's not looking, she tips the lot into the bin.'

The staff not only destroyed production equipment because it was an effective way of getting at the management, but because they had no qualms about doing so. As Alan said, 'It's got nothing to do with us, has it?'

Inaction

Inaction, a sin of omission rather than commission, was meant to lead to the deliberate destruction of raw materials, product, production equipment and non-production equipment: 16 cases were observed as having been carried out by the staff and 7 by the management.

Let the place burn

In the early hours of one Saturday morning, the staff discovered that a high voltage electrical transformer had started to smoulder. However, they did not disconnect the appliance from the mains, or inform the managers. It was only when a small, but potentially destructive, fire broke out that one of the group members went to find a manager.

The comments which the staff used to explain away their behaviour on this occasion were typical of those which would follow a case of inaction. For example, Ali said, 'I couldn't give a damn, let the bloody place burn down. It's nothing to do with me.' Sandra's reaction was: 'Oh to hell with it, I'm not going to go running to tell them every time something goes wrong, every time I see a little fire. It's their problem. If the place is really going to burn down, they'll find out soon enough and they can sort it out.'

An example of managerial inaction was that of a catering manager who was aware of a blockage in the drainage system underneath one of the bars and expressed his discontent with the General Manager – who was responsible for maintenance and repairs – by simply not informing him of the defect. As a result, the uncontrolled flow of waste water caused extensive damage to the building.

Even if the identities of those who were involved in cases of inaction were known, it was extremely difficult to prove that the inaction was deliberate. Those involved only had to plead ignorance of the event – for example, that they had not noticed that water was collecting under a washing machine or that the electric transformer was smouldering. In the case of the blocked drain, it was said that while the General Manager knew that the Catering Manager had kept it to himself, he realised that there was nothing he could do about it. He was annoyed about this and said, 'The next time he does that sort of thing I'll send him and his job down the bloody stairs'.

It was interesting to discover that the full consequences of inaction could not always be accurately predicted. For example, the staff on one particular bar kept complaining about a loose waste pipe on the washing machine, but to no avail. Eventually, and inevitably, the pipe finally came away altogether and the waste water started to flood the area. The staff decided to leave the Catering Manager to find out for himself.

The following evening it was discovered that the water had seeped through under the bar and damaged the expensive fitted carpet around the bar. As one of the staff explained later, 'We didn't know about the carpet, it's a shame really, I suppose, we just wanted to teach the manager a lesson.'

Not all the cases of inaction, on the part of the employees, were carried out against the management. In some cases the organisation itself became both the cause and the victim of inaction. For example, John, an experienced barman, described how he had been 'done' by customers three times in a row. Apparently they had left the bar without paying for their drinks. When John was asked what he had done about it, he said, 'Nothing, what could I do? I couldn't go around the place trying to find them amongst more than a thousand people. Anyway even if I did find them, it's none of my business. Who do you think would give a damn if I lost an eye in a fight? They'd just get somebody else to do the job. The truth is I'm fed up with this place.'

The observations at Alpha showed how the feelings of alienation and despair which originated from the work processes, created circumstances in which the participants – did not – or could not – identify their own interests with that of the organisation.

Wastage

Of the 14 cases which involved the wastage of raw materials, 13 were on the part of the staff and one was on the part of the managers. It was mostly beer and spirits which were deliberately wasted. For exmple, when Joe, a member of the bar staff, received a telephone call to the effect that his youngest child was ill and his wife had taken him to hospital, he asked the Catering Manager if he could leave and go to the hospital. The Catering Manager refused to give him permission. The Catering Manager was very abrupt and said, 'If you want to go, go but don't bother coming back if you do. You lot get paid to do a job. I couldn't care less, it's the business I am interested in not your kids. Don't waste my time again.'

Joe got his own back by adopting Sniper tactics. He explained how he added a measure of Pernod to several bottles of whisky, rum and brandy. All these spirits were ruined beyond redemption and had to be thrown away. The amount of profit which had been lost through this one act ran into hundreds of pounds. But as Joe said to his workmate, 'Do you think he's anything like as upset as I was last week? Fancy being responsible for all that waste, but that's nothing compared to what me and Helen went through with Todd. He's all right now, thank God (it had been a case of suspected meningitis), but what's my son's life compared to him and his profits?'

Destructive practices: Meanings and motives

Table 7

Destructive Practices	Managers' motives				Employees' motives			
	P	I	E	T	P	I	E	T
1. Raw materials	0	0	0	0	0	9	0	9
2. Production equipment	0	0	0	0	4	36	0	40
3. Product	0	0	0	0	0	1	0	1
4. Non-production equipment	0	0	0	0	0	4	0	4
5. Inaction	1	6	0	7	3	12	1	16
6. Wastage of raw materials	0	1	0	1	0	13	0	13
7. Wastage of non-production items	0	0	0	0	0	2	0	2
Total	1	7	0	8	7	77	1	85

P=Personal   I=Internal   E=External   T=Total

As shown in Table 7, of the 93 cases of destructive practices which were collected on the part of both the staff and the managers, 84 were internally motivated, 8 had personal motives and only one had an environmental motive.

The staff's main motives were those of frustration, tension and stress. Indeed, those groups of employees who were more likely to carry out destructive practices were those very groups on whom the most burdensome tasks fell. These groups were the bar staff, the kitchen staff and the glass-collectors. At certain periods, especially at the weekend, individuals in these groups could be subjected to a very high degree of stress. After one particularly busy night while Chris sat, looking pale and drained, waiting for her husband to come and collect her, she said, 'I just can't believe what tonight was like. It was a nightmare, a real nightmare. I do, I feel as if I've been asleep and I'm just waking up. My poor legs. All those people. And so hot and noisy. How many pints have I pulled tonight? You're serving one, as quickly as you can and you've got another twenty waiting and getting mad at you. And that's just at the bar. The rest are behind them, shouting and waving their money. And swearing at you. I don't know what is worse, the swearing or the crude comments.

'And then the managers. They push their way through that lot, come on to the bar, watch what's going on. They don't help at all. Oh no, not them. And then do you know what they say? It's incredible! They say you're not being chirpy enough. You've got to smile! At them! Those animals! They made me so mad, that when they'd toddled off I dropped a bottle of Tia Maria in the bin. A full one. Oohh, my legs, my head, all of me, I just want to go home and forget it till next week.'

While Chris had been feeling this way, Hassan and his fellow glass-collectors would also have been experiencing tension and frustration. At the height of a busy night, there would seldom be sufficient glasses. The bar staff and the managers would be exhorting the glass-collectors to find as many empty glasses as quickly as they could, but when the glass-collectors went to do as they were bid, they were often faced with the problem of people holding on to their drinks, even if they only had a drop left.

'I don't understand these people,' said Hassan. 'They don't want to give back their glasses. There was this old woman – white skirt, black see-through blouse and no bra. She had gin and tonic. She had four of them. Each in a different glass. I said, "Please, madam, my boss is after me. Those drinks could go in one glass. Please." She said to me, "That's not the way a lady drinks." I'm not believing my ears when she says that.

'And my poor friend Tariq, he's most upset. Tonight, he goes round collecting pint mugs the men leave around and forget. But he makes the big mistake. He goes down to the toilets and he is very happy. He sees six pint mugs. They look forgotten, they are all flat. They are in a row on the floor outside the toilets. He is coming back with them, quickly, when someone shouts. All these men, they are very cross. He gives back the drinks, he nearly gets punched, and my friend Tariq, he is only small. When he comes back up the stairs, the manager gets him. He asks, "What you doing, hiding in the toilets? Find some glasses!" He doesn't even see my friend is upset. Next week we're going to sort this place out.'

And they do. The following week Hassan and Tariq took turns to wash the glasses on a particular bar. On the subsequent evening it was discovered that the glass-washing machine they had been using was inoperable. 'Oh dear, now how we going to wash enough glasses to serve all those nice people?'

The managers, as noted earlier, rarely employed destructive practices as a means of getting even because they were held accountable and because they identified more than their staff did with the organisation's goals and objectives. Their main motives, however, when they did employ this sort of behaviour, were connected with the desire for more autonomy and attempts to discredit other people.

It was interesting to discover that although destructive practices did not result in material gain, they did offer some temporary satisfaction and relief which other forms of unconventional behaviour could not.

Styles

Table 8

Styles of destructive practice:	Lone Ranger	Sniper	Protester	Rebel
Managers	2	1	5	0
Employees	6	29	19	31

Destructive practices, in the main, were carried out in secret. This was obviously because the consequences of being caught would be grave. Most of the cases which were carried out openly by Lone Rangers and Protesters were those where it would be difficult to prove that a particular individual or group had been responsible. As we have already seen, this was particularly true of cases of inaction. Further, where wastage was concerned, it would also be difficult, if not impossible, to prove that the beers and spirits being poured down the sink, were really being wasted.

'Listen,' said Brian, 'if you really want to get the managers pissed off, this is what you do. Wait till they come to the bar and they're standing there with their friends. Right? Now you're busy serving. You pour a large round of drinks, say they want two lagers, two bitters, a whisky and lemonade, a brandy and coke and a gin and tonic? Right, well you pull five pints of lager and mix up the spirits, whisky and coke, brandy and lemonade and gin and lemonade. Now you can't keep those drinks to give to anyone else, because it doesn't look right, does it? So you have to pour three of the lagers away and the spirits and start again. The manager's going bonkers at the end of the bar, but he can't say anything. It's bloody great and he can't do a thing because all you've got to say is that we all make mistakes.'

Indeed, making deliberate mistakes was the most popular method of avoiding punishment amongst the bar staff when a case of wastage was suspected.

As can be seen from Table 8, the data concerning the staff's destructive practices, when carried out covertly, were just as likely to be done by a Sniper or by Rebels.

Where pilferage was concerned, we observed that Rebel action was a popular means of getting even. The reason for this was that it was generally felt that there was safety in numbers. However, where destructive practices were concerned, the style in which it was carried out was much more likely to be determined by whether or not the grievance which prompted the action was a personal or shared one.

In this chapter we have seen many examples of Sniper action. Luke, Roberto, Chris, Joe, John and the Catering Manager had personal reasons, while the bar staff watched as a fire began to break out; and Hassan and Tariq shared feelings of anger and frustration and linked up in a joint attempt to get even. Here is a further example of Rebel action.

Where did they get their glasses?

New pint mugs which were issued to the bars were thought to be particularly awkward to work with. They were old-fashioned and had no rims. 'You never get a head on them and customers say they don't want the drink, because it's flat. Where *did* they get these glasses?', asked Neil.

The bar staff agreed that the pint mugs were difficult to stack up on the narrow shelves behind the bars. The group of five bar staff who worked on the Bermuda bar discovered that if the traditional heavy mugs were stacked on top of the new ones, the new ones soon became chipped and unusable. 'Just imagine,' said Marcia to a close friend; 'if all the glasses are stacked this way we'll soon get rid of them!' And so they did.

The reasons for adopting Rebel tactics are manifold. It was not always the seriousness with which the nature of the action was regarded that warranted the use of this style. Indeed, the most horrendous acts of destruction in the work environment have been seen to involve only one individual, for example, the contamination of baby foods.

Rebel action would at times be used if the nature of the action to be taken demanded the involvement of more than one person, or if the members of a group were sufficiently cohesive to feel that one member's grievance was a cause for them all to act. For example, when Alpha's management decided to slim down the overheads, two of the cleaners were laid off. The General Manager's remark that 'too many Mrs Mopps are knocking about', did not please the cleaning ladies. They decided that they would all quit together but not before 'teaching the General Manager a good lesson – something to remember us by'.

On the following Monday morning, the General Manager walked in to see Alpha's famous wooden dance floor thoroughly soaked, with four mops and buckets left standing in the middle. Despite the efforts made to save the dance floor, nearly one-third of the floor tiles had to be replaced and as the General Manager put it, 'It's never been the same since.'

Summary

Destructive practices can be separated into three distinct categories: destruction, inaction and wastage.

Employees are more likely to carry out acts of destruction than managers. Managers do not favour this means of getting even for three main reasons. Firstly, they are held accountable for any damage to the organisation's property. Secondly, they are aware that being held responsible for a destructive act would wreak untold damage to their careers. Thirdly, their identification with the goals and objectives of the organisation inhibits them from taking part in acts of destruction.

Managers are not so reluctant, however, to indulge in inaction. This is because they know, as do employees, that it is very difficult to prove culpability in cases of inaction.

Again, and in common with destruction, wastage is more likely to be carried out by employees than by managers.

The motives for destructive practices by the employees and, in relatively few cases, by the managers, derived from within the organisation. Destructive practices, in the main, were carried out covertly by either Snipers or Rebels. Those cases of destructive practices which were carried out openly, by Lone Rangers or Protesters, were those cases which concerned inaction, where it would be difficult to prove that a particular individual or group had been responsible.

6

NON-COOPERATION

In a medium-sized engineering firm in the North-East, the management refused a demand for a 9.6 per cent wage rise. Instead they offered a 7.6 per cent increase. The shop steward, Jack, relayed the offer to the work-force and also added that the managers had suggested that, as they were in an area of high unemployment, the offer should be considered carefully.

In this case the staff felt that they had no real choice but to accept the offer. Six months later 'Engineering Ltd' received a foreign order for 500 water pumps. This was an order from which the firm could benefit enormously, but which would require the full cooperation of its employees, for without overtime the order would not be completed in time. Jack told the management that he was almost certain that without bonuses he could not get the workforce to agree to work overtime on a rush job of that size. 'You see, the lads are still upset about what happened six months back. But I'll do my best . . .' However, after a week Jack came back with the bad news that overtime 'was out of the question'.

This form of behaviour constitutes one of the most subtle forms of getting even. When the achievement of certain objectives depends on the co-operation of individuals and groups, they can get even by the simple expedient of *not* cooperating. Non cooperation is distinct from rule-breaking in that cooperation is sometimes required to meet objectives which are outside the boundaries of an individual's or group's normal and designated work roles. That is, if there is a rule stating that people should keep their particular work area tidy and they do not, then they are rule-breaking. However, if people are only requested to keep their bench or desk tidy and they do not, then they are just not co-operating. Further, if someone breaks a rule, their superiors are then in a position to mete out a suitable punishment. However, when people fail to cooperate there is little, at least officially, that can be done.

Table 9

Areas of non-cooperation	Management	Employees
General	2	28
Raw materials	0	2
Production equipment	1	0
Product	1	1
Product time	0	7
Total	4	38

At Alpha, and perhaps not surprisingly, cases of non-cooperation would most commonly occur when the managers expected the unquestioning cooperation of the staff. Of the 42 cases which were recorded, 38 were carried out by the staff and only 4 by the managers.

Employees and non-cooperation

Owing to their respective positions in the organisation's hierarchy, the managers expected that the staff would cooperate with them, that they, 'should do as they're told', and 'not answer back'. When this cooperation was not always forthcoming, they would be perplexed. As Tim, a catering manager said, 'I just don't get it when they let you down. It makes no sense at all. In any game you sometimes have to do a bit more than usual. And you've got to have a boss and you've got to have staff and they have to do what they're told or else there's no point. Then you're on your way to anarchy.'

However, the staff believed that they were justified in not always cooperating with the managers. They believed that as they were paid low wages to do an unpleasant job during unsociable hours, they should not be asked to undertake extra responsibilities.

The following is a memorable case of non-cooperation in that it involved almost all of the staff.

Get the place shipshape

One Friday at midnight, the managers received a message to the effect that the Directors would visit the branch at 8 p.m. the following evening. The General Manager decided to call an emergency meeting. No one was to go home, but had to wait around until the whole staff had finished their respective tasks and had assembled. The staff had been working from 7.45 p.m. and by 3 a.m., in the early hours of Saturday morning, all the staff wanted to do was to go home. However, on this particular occasion they were not able to leave the club until 4 a.m. The General Manager spoke to them at great length about the importance of the visit. Two cleaners had been dismissed by him for 'fiddling' and so he was asking the staff to help get everything shipshape.

'I want all of you, without exception, to be here at half past six. I'm relying on you, don't let me down. It's very important for me. Let's get here and get the place cleaned up.'

He then allowed the staff to go home. It was a mutinous band of people who started to make their way homewards. They had been subjected to heat, noise, pressure and toil for more than six hours. Many of the staff had not had a break. At

3 a.m. they wanted nothing more than to go home and get to bed. Finally, it was only with difficulty that a number of staff were able to find transport home in the early hours of the morning. Many had to rely on the infrequent night bus service and would now have to wait for at least an hour in the dangerous city centre streets. Some of the women felt that they had no alternative but to hire a taxi, a safer but more expensive alternative. Other female staff were collected by fathers, husbands or boyfriends, which meant that the latter had been obliged to wait while the General Manager 'spouted off'.

Chris was particularly upset. Her husband, who also worked a full day, had to leave their home at 2.30 in the morning, their children asleep in their beds, drive as quickly as possible to Alpha, collect Chris and then drive back. The whole procedure would take forty-five minutes and caused both Chris and her husband a great deal of anxiety. They did not like to leave their children unattended, but there was no bus service which went near their house. However, as they had a mortgage to pay off, they relied heavily on not only what Chris earned but also what she could acquire in gratuities. After being kept waiting for nearly an hour, Chris was almost in tears: 'Look here, it's not just me now, is it? Jim's been waiting here to take me home and he's had to leave the kids on their own. Anything could have happened by now. I can't and I'm not, coming in at that time tomorrow. I want to see my kids. He's just asking too much.'

Other people felt just as angry and upset at being delayed, like Mandy: 'I've missed my bus now. I don't know when there'll be another one. And I'm supposed to be helping my mum out at the shop. I have to be up at 7 again. I'm not letting her down, but there's no point in my going to bed now. I'm coming in at my usual time tomorrow. I'll get some rest at tea-time. Stuff him.'

And Luke: 'Come here, come here again! At that time? There's no point in going home is there? What does he think we are?'

And Ali: 'Who's he talking to like that? We're not rubbish. Making me late home. He wants the place clean? He can do it himself. He sacked the cleaners, not me!'

And Linda: 'He's got a bloody cheek! We've been rushed off our feet all night. Put up with rudeness, swearing, God knows what, does he say thanks? No, he bloody doesn't! Just come in and work like bloody slaves! Well, he can forget it.'

Needless to say, very few people turned up at 6.30 the next evening, and those who did only did so reluctantly. As staff came in to work, they were set to tidying and cleaning up, but they only did this half-heartedly. As a result, when the Directors made their visit, an hour later than arranged, it was to be met by a disgruntled atmosphere and a less than shipshape night club. The General Manager, clearly in a predicament, was heard to say, 'The cleaners have let us down today and the staff have done their best.'

When the managers attempted to discover why it was that most of the staff had not cooperated with the General Manager's request, they were met by a wall of unanswerable excuses. Chris: 'I had to wait for Jim to get home from work to bring me in. I tried to come on the bus, but I couldn't get anyone to mind the kids.' Mandy: 'I had to wait for my dad to bring me.' Luke: 'I thought there was a bus at ten past, but there wasn't. I had to wait.' Ali: '6.30? I thought you said 7.30. Sorry.' Linda: 'Tonight? Oh dear. I thought it was next week. Aren't I daft?'

In some cases the managers' demands were followed by some form of subtle and direct intimidation. For example, when last-minute arrangements were made for a function for a party of 600 employees of a local company, Sigma, on a Sunday night, the General Manager announced the news the night before.

'I wonder if you know about Sigma's annual party night? We're extremely lucky that they've come to us this year. I know it's tomorrow, but there's nothing I can do about it. I expect everyone, without exception, to come to work tomorrow (a

Sunday night when generally Alpha was closed) at 6 o'clock. This 'do' means a lot to us. I'd like us to get the Branch of the Year Award. I'm relying on your cooperation and of course we'll remember who it is who gives us a hand at times like this. That's all.'

On this occasion again, the staff were angry and resentful. They resented the idea that they had nothing better to do with their Sundays than to work at the Alpha. Like most people the staff had already made commitments to family and friends or were simply looking forward to a quiet, relaxing day. To be expected suddenly to break these arrangements infuriated many of the staff – Tina, for example: 'I've got everybody coming over to Sunday lunch tomorrow. I can't just drop it.'

Many of the staff felt that when they were expected to work an extra session, particularly on a Sunday, they should be given sufficient warning of at least a week.

The fact that the General Manager also appeared to be making some sort of veiled threat provoked further negative reactions, for instance from Sue: 'What did he mean by that? They'll remember us if we help out? What on earth is that supposed to mean? What'll happen if we don't? I don't like the sound of that at all.'

On that particular Sunday night more than half of the staff did not turn up and most of those who did were late.

Most cases of non-cooperation on the part of the staff were of this type, i.e. not turning up at times which, although they had been asked to, were not, strictly speaking, within the normal course of their duties. This sort of non-cooperation could also be seen to apply to much more than just being late; it was a deliberate attempt to get even with the management by resisting their authority through non-cooperation.

More specific instances were those which could be clearly linked to raw materials, production equipment, product and production time. Production time refers to the time that an individual should normally have been working. As we can see from Table 9, non-cooperation at these times was also quite popular.

99

If specifically requested to come to work on time, people could be late, or if asked to take less than the twenty minutes allowed for breaks, just as they were leaving the bar, could deliberately wait until they would normally have returned.

Managers and non-cooperation

As we learnt earlier from Tim, the Catering Manager, the managers held different attitudes from the staff towards extra work. Whilst staff believed that 'You don't do a damn thing more than you have to in this place' (Brian), the managers acted as if they believed that they should always do, or at least be seen to do, as much as they could to further the interests of the organisation.

Kevin, a catering manager: 'I don't see this just as a job, it's my career. And this club, it's not just where I work, I've a lot of responsibility here, I look after it like it's my own place. If there's anything I can do to make things better, of course, I'll do it. Look at last week: I spent my day off in here going through the stock.'

Jed, an assistant catering manager: 'Of course, you do anything they ask. I want to get to the top of the tree and I know which side my bread's buttered on.'

Cooperating, where the managers were concerned, did mean that quite often they had to overlook their basic differences of opinion, either with each other or with their superiors. However, as the four cases which *were* collected indicates, this was not always possible.

An assistant catering manager was talking about what had happened to Dave, the latest in a long line of catering managers. 'Dave was very keen on being efficient. He wanted to get the stock-sheets exactly right. Now, we all know we can't have it exactly right don't we? If it's *exactly* right, down to the last penny, where are the little perks of the job going to come from? Mr Bond, our beloved General Manager, didn't like it one little bit, having Dave breathing down his neck with the accounts in one hand and his calculator – a scientific one, no less – in the other. So the Area Supervisor pops in to look at the books and there's Dave all smiles and dead pleased with himself, the figures aren't right, but they're a heck of a lot better than they've been. But when the man asks for them, no books. Can't find the bloody things anywhere. Dave was practically on his knees, begging Bond to remember where they were. His comment was, "Oh you need *my* cooperation now do you?"'

Of course, the books were 'found' in the end, but it was too late for Dave. Dave continued to be a particularly sharp thorn in the General Manager's side and was soon sent on to pastures new.

The following is an example of managerial non-cooperation in another organisation, Posher's Disco.

'Talk about letting your boss down. I've seen some things in my time but this beats the lot of them. Some time ago, about ten months I think, we had a visit from the Fire Inspector. Well the exit doors were locked and so of course we got a telling-off and a caution. I was told that if it happened again they'd throw the book at us. But just imagine leaving the fire doors open to the car park on a busy Saturday night! They'd be through the doors before you could blink. I'd have to have a bouncer on each one and then there'd be no one at the main entrance.

'Anyway, it had to happen, didn't it? The other night Tommy, my assistant, rang me up from the box-office and said the fire inspectors were here. I flew down the stairs and got the keys off Beverley, the catering manageress, to open the doors, but they were the wrong blasted keys. What is it with these catering managers and manageresses? They always seem to have it in for me. We got done of course and when I asked Miss High-and-Mighty what she had been playing at, she just laughed and said, "You don't mean that you actually *wanted* to break the law, do you?"'

Non-cooperation: Meanings and motives

Table 10

Non-cooperative practices	Managers' motives				Employees' motives			
	P	I	E	T	P	I	E	T
General	0	2	0	2	7	20	1	28
Raw materials	0	0	0	0	0	2	0	2
Production equipment	0	1	0	1	0	0	0	0
Product	0	1	0	1	0	1	0	1
Production time	0	0	0	0	0	7	0	7
Total	0	4	0	4	7	30	1	38

P=Personal   I=Internal   E=External   T=Total

As we have seen above, non-cooperation would be used when one individual or group wished, as a means of getting even, to make it difficult for another individual or group to achieve one or more certain objectives.

As shown in Table 10, on the rare occasions when the managers resorted to non-cooperative practices, the motives they attributed to their actions originated from within the organisation. Most of the employees' motives, as we have seen in the cases above, likewise derived from the organisation, though some were also attributed to Personal and External sources.

As we have seen in the case concerning Dave, the Catering Manager, and Mr Bond, the General Manager, managers could use non-cooperation as a means of discrediting other people. The desire for more status and for profit maximisation were also reasons for not cooperating with others.

In contrast, staff would not cooperate with the management when they felt frustrated or wished to challenge authority.

Indeed, it was the basic antagonism existing between the staff and the managers which would ignite feelings of frustration and a desire to challenge authority, sparked off when the managers asked the employees to cooperate with them.

Whenever the Chancellor put up the price of beer and 'shorts' by two pence, the staff would know that this would create problems in terms of the customers' reactions. Alpha's price list would show an increase of ten pence per pint and between fifteen and twenty pence for spirits, regardless of whether the present stocks had been used up or not. This would infuriate the customers and the more belligerent among them would start arguments with the staff. At such times the staff were always reminded that, should a disagreement occur, the management would explain the situation to the customer. Bridie had such an experience one night: 'They said the prices were dear. I said I agree but there's nothing I can do about it. That's how it is, the managers set the prices, we only sell the stuff. The bastard said I was an "Irish thickie". I could have murdered him. I sent Judy for the Manager. After a good ten minutes he turned up and apologised to the bastards! He said, "Give the lads a drink on the house." Could you believe that? I said that I expected support from the management. He said the customers pay for your and my wages. They're always right. Great, isn't it? They expect your cooperation but they never stand behind you, do they?'

Other people expressed similar feelings. Tamsin: 'What a cheek! They treat you like muck most of the time and then they expect you to drop everything and do what they want.' Hussein: 'It makes me very angry. I am told to do this, do that, no please, no thank you, then it is, "Please Hussein, you do this for me." I think the man is mad. He treats me bad and then when he wants something, he is all very nice. I think, "So, you want something now, want me to do this little favour? No sir, I'm not doing it". And I don't.' Alex: 'The job's awful, the place is a dump, the managers look at you as if you've crawled out of the bog, but I put up with it for the money, and I can work during the day as well as night. All them rules, OK, I stick to them, but there's no way I'm doing more than I have to. I'm not working extra nights or nothing. It's not worth it to me, not with the tax, and they can't make you. Let them just try it.'

The staff would also use non-cooperation as a strategy for getting even when they wished to exert control over what happened in the workplace.

A prize for the best costume

As was customary the staff had been asked to attire themselves in costumes which were appropriate for Hallowe'en. Those familiar with the night-club industry will know that fancy dress is typical of the sort of gimmick used to attract more customers. The managers informed the staff that there was to be a better prize than usual for the best costume.

Tara, who was to some better known as 'Miss Erotica', and who had walked off with the prize for the last two years running, was full of enthusiasm. 'Oh, that will be fun!'

However, when other members of the staff discussed Hallowe'en, on the bars and at their coffee-breaks, it became clear that they felt less than enthusiastic. Eventually most people decided that for once they were not going to make idiots of themselves. Many of the female staff were particularly indignant because they felt that the prize was not awarded to the person who had shown the most ingenuity, but, as Nina said, to 'Anyone who's got enough cheek to show off their knickers and as much as they can of their boobs without getting arrested'.

Tara's costumes had indeed been somewhat revealing on the two occasions on which she had won the prize. Maria added, 'When the customers see her dressed like that, they think we're all easy . . . and the bloody managers encourage her. It's bloody disgusting.'

On that Hallowe'en, none of the staff came to work 'dressed up' except Miss Erotica. She won both the prize and, as Maria politely put it, the admiration of the management.

Styles

Table 11

Non-cooperation	Lone Ranger	Sniper	Protester	Rebel
Managers	2	0	0	2
Employees	4	9	16	9

As we discussed earlier, it was only on rare occasions that managers would not cooperate with the demands made on them by their superiors or each other. The four cases which were collected, however, did not provide us with sufficient evidence to assert with any certainty that the managers preferred any particular style when they did fail to cooperate.

As Table 11 above shows, the most popular style in which the style would not cooperate was as Protesters. The reasons for this are twofold. As we saw in one of the above cases, the managers would quite often, and at very short notice, ask a group of people to work an extra night in order to cater for a private function. At least some of the staff were always incensed by this cavalier attitude. They would then quite openly fail to cooperate because they felt that they were in the right and could therefore not be punished with any justification.

Chris: 'Look, they have to give you some notice. The night before is no use. Anybody'd agree that we're right. We're not just going to turn up every time they say. And just let them try and do anything about it. We'd go to those people, what are they called? Some tribunal? See what they have to say about it. You look at your contract and see what it has to say about working extra nights at a moment's notice. Nothing, that's what, not a dickie bird.'

There were other occasions when the staff would be quite open about the fact that they were not going to cooperate with the managers. For example, during slack periods the bar staff would sometimes be asked to set to and spring-clean the bars. They would be up in arms about this.

Mandy to Tim, a catering manager: 'You've got to be joking. You don't really expect us to get on our hands and knees and start cleaning? What are the cleaners for? You wouldn't ask them to come behind the bar and start serving drinks, would you? So why do you think that we should be doing their job? None of us are budging. When we get customers we'll serve them and when there's glasses to wash we'll wash them. We're doing our own job and nobody else's.'

However, as Table 11 shows, the staff did not always feel that they could be quite so open about not cooperating with the managers. Eighteen cases of non-cooperation were carried out covertly, nine by Snipers and the other nine by Rebels.

The following two cases illustrate firstly, Sniper and secondly, Rebel action.

A pain in the neck

According to Maria, the new glass-washing machines were 'a pain in the neck': 'The soap keeps trickling inside and it's even harder than washing the bloody things in the sinks. Useless they are. They're making our job even harder. You've got to wash the bloody things and then take them to the other end and rinse them off. What a palaver. You know what the Catering Manager said to us, "Do it for me, girls." What? I wouldn't do it for me old man. Who does he think he is? I never drink from their glasses. I've got my own. Have you seen them customers kissing and carrying on and all that? Puhh! Sip from them glasses and you *will* be sorry. Don't tell me that washing can clean those germs. No chance.'

Jerry gets a pasting

Jerry, the current Catering Manager, had warned the bar staff to look out for a group of five lads who had perfected a con trick. They would approach a bar at a busy period and order several drinks. Then before they were served with the final one they would simply melt into the crowd. It was believed that this organised group visited different clubs on a random basis in order to avoid being recognised or barred.

Mickey, the door supervisor, explained what happened when Jerry finally caught up with the gang: 'The club was packed, nobody could move, nearly 2,000 customers were sardined in here. Joey from the corner bar managed to get through to tell us that Jerry had found them. We weren't very happy with Jerry just then. I don't know whether you know, but he stopped us door supervisors from having a drink, even when it was paid for by one of the regulars. Besides, he had said we were useless. So when Joey came for us we decided to take our time. But when we got there things were worse than we'd thought. The thieving bastards were kicking the daylights out of him. We sorted it out. Jerry was a mess. Anyway, he's lucky he's not dead.'

Summary

Non-cooperation can occur when managers and employees are requested to undertake tasks and responsibilities which are outside the normal work role.

Managers are less likely than employees to fail to cooperate. Members of the management identify with organisational objectives to the extent where they will endeavour to overcome their differences in order to achieve organisational goals. Employees, however, do not identify so strongly with organisational goals. Indeed, when asked to cooperate in order to achieve specific objectives, employees can use the opportunity to inhibit the attainment of these goals and thus get even with the management.

The relatively few cases of non-cooperation which were carried out on the part of the managers had motives which originated within the organisation. The reasons for non-cooperation on the part of the staff also derived from internal sources. Insufficient cases were collected of non-cooperation by the managers to be able to determine with any degree of confidence whether or not a particular style would be preferred when they do not wish to cooperate. The most popular style which the staff would adopt when they did not wish to cooperate was a Protester's.

7

DISRUPTIVE PRACTICES

A large wedding reception was being held at one of London's grander hotels when pandemonium broke out. The bride's mother let out a dreadful scream and then fainted. Then one of the bridesmaids, pale with terror, yelled, 'It's a mouse! It's just jumped out of the crackers!'

She climbed onto her chair, holding her voluminous skirts up above her knees. Chaos ensued while the men of the party tried to calm the ladies and to find the uninvited guest. However, they searched to no avail and as the ladies would not, indeed could not, resume their meal while the creature might still be within the vicinity, the wedding meal had to be abandoned and the guests moved to the room where the disco was to take place.

In the aftermath of this event the bride's father refused to honour the hotel's bill and the hotel manager was a much sadder and wiser man: 'I can't prove it, but I've a damned good idea who did it and why. Two of the waiters wanted the night off to go to some pop concert with their girlfriends and I said, no, they had to do the wedding reception.'

Disruptive practices are those means by which individuals and groups can create a disturbance or commotion in the work environment. As the cases included in this chapter will show, disruptive practices can take various forms and range from a minor disturbance which only involves one or two people to a major event which affects the whole organisation.

SABOTAGE

At Alpha the 36 cases of disruptive practices which were collected were all carried out by the staff. As in many organisations, at Alpha there were slack periods when there was little to do and the employees became bored and restless. We found that it was at these – though by no means the only – times that disruptive practices were most likely to take place. The following two cases are examples of just how the staff at Alpha and at a branch of a nationwide supermarket were able to relieve their boredom by causing a commotion.

Let's have some fun

One quiet Wednesday night the staff on one of the bars decided to have some 'fun'. When most of the customers who were standing at the bar went onto the dance floor, Heather wiped the top of the bar and at the same time swopped the customers' drinks about. Ali, lounging against his till, watched what she was doing and then moved forward and removed two of the glasses altogether, tipped the contents down the sink and washed them. When the customers returned to the bar a great deal of confusion ensued. No one could find their drinks and they began to argue among themselves as to which drink belonged to whom. Eventually Dave, the current Catering Manager, was asked to come to the bar. The customers were finally pacified when he, reluctantly, said that they could have a free round of drinks. The bar staff watched these proceedings with hidden glee.

Sale time

The manager of a large supermarket belonging to a nationwide chain of stores told us what happened in his branch when business was quiet one wet and dreary Monday morning.

The supermarket, as usual, had been open since 8.30 and by 9.30 only three of the eight cashiers had served one or two people. It was about this time that the store manager was making his rounds before going to sit in his office with a pot of coffee and the morning papers. He noticed that there was some desultory chat going on across the three end tills. He realised that they were bored but then, as he said, working on a till was scarcely the most exciting job in the world.

An hour later, whilst reading the paper, he became aware of the sound of shouting coming from the direction of the cash tills and he went to investigate. The scene which met his eyes made his blood run cold. He saw that a crowd of shoppers – who seemed to have appeared from nowhere – and staff had congregated round one of the tills and that they all seemed to be watching something with avid interest. One of the supervisors, flushed and close to tears, was engaged in a heated argument with a lady shopper who was also red in the face, but extremely angry. She was grimly hanging onto her shopping basket which the manager saw, to his horror, contained several tins of salmon and other expensive items all bearing the store's green 'Half Marked Price' label.

When the manager was eventually able to find out what had happened, it appeared that a person or persons unknown, but obviously a member of staff, had managed to get hold of the roll of green 'Half Marked Price' tickets. They had then proceeded to add to the wire bin reserved for half price goods some of the supermarket's more expensive items. It appeared that this had been done during the slack time while the supervisors were in the staff room. This particular supervisor had come to tell the check-out staff that they should take their breaks earlier, when she noticed that an exultant lady had a basket full of half-priced goods. The supervisor thought that this was very odd. When she saw that the lady's shopping basket contained half-price salmon and other expensive groceries, she realised that something was very wrong indeed. These were items which would never find their way to the half-price bin. She had tried to retrieve the goods from the customer, explaining that some dreadful mistake had been made. Unfortunately for the supervisor, the lady shopper was not a timid being who was going to hand over meekly her booty. As she said many times, over and over again, she knew her rights. If that was the price they had on them, mistake or no mistake, by law that was the price they had to be sold at and that was the price she was going to pay; or else.

When the manager intervened and tried to appeal to the lady's good nature, he found it was to no avail. She threatened to telephone everyone from the Trading Standards Office to the *That's Life* programme. She then took a pen and notebook out of her voluminous handbag and started asking people for their names and addresses so that she could quote them as witnesses, if necessary.

The manager felt that he had no option but to let the customer have the goods at half the marked price. He even tried to smile magnanimously and to imply that the supervisor had made a mistake. Of course, he never found out exactly who was responsible.

As with all forms of getting even, the staff and operatives have found that disruptive practices are an effective way of getting at the management. Some of the cases observed were indirectly carried out against the managers who might or might not have to sort out the resulting confusion. Others, as the following case illustrates, were carried out directly against the managers.

To stop you lot fiddling

One evening the bar staff arrived at work to find that bright lights had been installed over the tills. When they approached the Catering Manager and asked him why the bright lights had been put in, his reply was, 'To stop you lot fiddling. The stocks are down and I suspect that it's your bar which is responsible.' The bar staff were upset because they felt that they had been humiliated in front of everyone.

That weekend the Catering Manager was called to the bar countless times to rectify the 'mistakes' that the bar staff had made in registering the price of the rounds they had served. The bar staff said that they could not help it – the lights were so bright that they were glaring on the till buttons. The following week when the staff came into work, they found that the lights had been restored to their former state. That weekend normal service was resumed and the staff did not make any 'mistakes'. Unfortunately for the Catering Manager, they also went home that weekend with 'enough money to make up for what we lost last week with those damn lights'.

As we saw in Chapter 3, pilferage could often be used as a means of compensating those concerned for whatever it was they felt that they had lost. This was just such a case.

In another incident, the management were called to 'sort out the mess' down in the basement where the cloakrooms were located. More than 500 articles of clothing, including fur coats and expensive leather jackets, had been hung on the wrong hangers by a discontented employee who had then quit her job. It took more than two and a half hours to match the articles with the descriptions given by their owners.

Apart from the disruption which had been caused, eight customers had to be compensated for articles which were never found, including four fur coats. These items had been conveniently placed in the front row and were therefore visible to any opportunists who could then describe them accurately and claim them as their own.

As the foregoing demonstrates, disruptive practices could be very effective as a means of getting even. However, in common with inaction which was discussed in Chapter 5, disruption could sometimes have unpredicted and unwelcome consequences. The following is a good example of just how this method of getting even could become unmanageable. The consequence can only be described as horrifying – it had certainly not been predicted or intended.

Havoc and mayhem

It was a very hectic Friday night and as usual the glass-collectors were being hounded by both the Catering Manager and the bar staff to find and bring as many glasses to the bar as possible. On this particular evening two of the glass collectors, Jim and Amir, were feeling more aggravated than usual. They felt that Kevin, the Catering Manager, was 'picking on' them. They decided to do something about it.

Both the bar staff and the glass-collectors found that swopping the customers' drinks about whilst the customers were away dancing, or removing them altogether, was a good way of causing a commotion. It would usually cause no more than a spate of grumbling and a trip to the bar to buy a fresh round of drinks. As in the case above the managers would sometimes become involved as well. On this particular occasion Amir and Jim chose to swop glasses about in their attempt to get even. Their intention in carrying out this action was to have some 'fun' at the customers' expense and to get some glasses to take back to the bar.

When Amir and Jim saw that a large group of men who were occupying a number of tables were celebrating a stag night, they decided that they should be the victims of their practical joke. Amir and Jim waited until the members of the stag party had reached a state of advanced inebriation and then put their plan into action. They slipped in between the tables and while apparently removing the empty glasses and emptying the ashtrays into a small bin, swopped several of the drinks about, between the tables as well as on them. The men were too inebriated, or too busy chatting up the ladies or discussing the 'talent', to notice the activities of the two glass-collectors. Jim and Amir then stood by and waited for the fun to begin.

Unfortunately the situation soon became critical. It appeared that one of the tables had not, as Amir and Jim believed, been occupied by members of the stag party, but by other customers. One of the stag party, in the search for his drink became convinced that it was on that particular table and accused one of the large and brawny men sitting there of stealing it. A verbal altercation followed and the air turned blue with abuse. And then the first punch was thrown and before the two glass-collectors knew what had happened, fighting had broken out which quickly escalated until it seemed as if the whole night-club was one mass of flailing arms and legs. The bouncers soon realised that they would not be able to contain the fight on their own and the police were called. No sooner had the white-faced General Manager called the police than he was back in his office telephoning for an ambulance.

Some of the people involved in the fight had been seriously injured. One man had been trampled on. It took two vanloads of policemen to break up the fight and two ambulances to deal with the injured. Even then it was not over. There was the aftermath to cope with. Despite what had happened and the damage which had been done to the night-club, the band carried on playing and the staff were expected to continue as though nothing had happened.

Unfortunately, it was rather difficult to continue as if nothing had happened. The ambulance men had only removed the seriously injured; those with superficial wounds had been left to nurse them as best they could. Some of the people remained in the night-club and carried on drinking and behaved as if nothing had happened. This shocked and horrified the staff, as people were coming to the bar covered in blood and ordering drinks.

'It was awful', said Gina. 'I couldn't believe it. It was like my worst nightmares about this place. Did you see what I had to serve? There was this bloke, his shirt was in shreds, and what there was of it was soaked in blood. He had this gash on his forehead and blood was coming out of it and he just stood there and asked for two pints of bitter. They were so drunk that they couldn't even go and clean themselves up.'

When the glass-collectors began to clear up the mess and bring the broken and bloodied glasses to the bar, the staff were upset yet again.

'I was sick', said Chris. 'I had to go to the Ladies and be sick. The glass-collectors were looking pretty green as well, they were bringing glasses to the bar with blood on them and bits in them. I couldn't take it, it was awful, dreadful, unbelievable.'

This case was the most dramatic in terms of events getting beyond the control of the initiators, but it aptly illustrates what can happen when employees set out merely to have a bit of fun. It was this unpredictability which rendered disruptive practices less popular than other forms of getting even. Note that during six years only 36 cases were collected at Alpha.

Disruptive practices: Meanings and motives

Table 12

Employees' motives

	P	I	E	Total
Disruptive practices	6	30	0	36

P=Personal   I=Internal   E=External

As can be seen from Table 12, thirty cases had motives which were attributable to the organisation and six had motives which were personal.

Where the motives were attributable to the organisation, the staff said that they had engaged in disruptive practices because they wanted more control over their work; they were seeking revenge; they were bored; or because they were angry.

It was the desire for revenge which provided the motivation in two of the cases above, where the Catering Manager changed the lights above the tills and where Jim and Amir swopped the customers' drinks. In the case where Heather and Ali swopped the drinks around and disposed of two of them altogether, they said that they had done this because they were bored. In Ali's word, 'Look, it was dead, no customers, so we got to do something to make the night pass, it was just so boring.'

In those cases where the motives were personal, those involved professed to have been bored; to have had the desire for some 'fun' and 'thrills'.

The following is an example of a case which had personal motives.

Where's the Ladies?

A subsidiary stockroom for spirits was located next to the Ladies powder-room. It was not unusual for the female customers to mistake the stockroom for the powder-room and to accidentally walk into it when the door was open. One night the sound of frantic screaming could be heard from within the stockroom. After a few minutes the barman who had last used the stockroom was found. However, as he could not remember where he had put the keys and nobody else was able to locate them the door had to be forced open and the terrified customer released. When an explanation was sought, the barman claimed that he was unaware that someone had gone inside the room so he had switched off the lights and shut the door.

Later he confided to a close friend, 'It livened up this place, a bit of excitement. One minute it was boring and the next she was screaming her head off because she couldn't find the light switch. Do you think the managers would break down the door if one of us was trapped in there? No bloody chance!'

Apart from attempting to relieve their boredom, it was also discovered that the staff had more fundamental reasons for occasionally resorting to disruptive actions. They were aware that their jobs as bar staff, kitchen staff, glass-collectors and so on were exactly the kind which are described as unfulfilling and 'dead-end' jobs. At times they would be overwhelmed by the hopeless reality of their situation and filled with feelings of helplessness and frustration. It was at times when there was nothing to do that harsh reality was most likely to rear its ugly head and it was for this reason that the workers would do anything to kill time. As Tina said, 'If you start thinking, you've had it. It makes you proper fed up when you can't see any way out.'

In order to avoid the dangers of thinking, there was a host of practices which were used to relieve boredom. Filling in football coupons, reminiscing and gossiping were among the most popular. Then, if everything else failed, disruptive practices were always a further option.

Styles

Table 13

Style of disruption:	Lone Ranger	Sniper	Protester	Rebel
Employees	0	5	1	30

As can be seen from Table 13, Rebel actions were responsible for most cases of disruptive practices. Indeed, all the cases which we have employed in this chapter were carried out by Rebels, with two exceptions: one was the only case which was carried out by Protesters and concerned the lights over the tills; the other was the Sniper case, where a female customer was locked in the spirit stockroom.

Disruptive practices were mostly carried out by Rebels for two main reasons. Firstly, those involved felt that if the managers knew who had caused the disruption they would not have been looked on too favourably and that therefore this was a means of getting even which should be carried out covertly.

'Dave was hopping mad, wasn't he?' said Heather. 'I got a bit worried there. I thought he might think it was us. If he did, he might have made us pay for the drinks. We wouldn't be laughing then, would we? Crying more like! There must have been about twenty customers he had to let have free drinks.'

Secondly, this form of getting even was one which would normally require at least two people to carry it out successfully. For example, one person would be needed to act as a lookout while the other person or persons set the chain of events in motion. The manager of the supermarket was convinced that at least two people had been responsible for that particular disruption. He told us that one person would have been needed to keep an eye on the doors leading to the staff room and to his office, and at least one more person to actually carry out the deed.

Of course, these Rebel actions could not have come to fruition if those involved had not initially shared feelings of, for example, boredom. In five cases of Sniper action, we found that either no such consensus of opinion had been reached or those concerned simply wished to act alone. However, causing a disruption single-handed is technically more difficult. The following case of Sniper action illustrates the extent to which someone acting alone would have to plan the disruption while ensuring that their identity would remain secret.

Bomb hoax

The management decided to increase the mid-week sessions on Tuesday, Wednesday and Thursday, from five to six hours per night. This would mean that employees would have to go home later and their previous routines would be upset.

It was also discovered that the management had decided to terminate the employment of those members of staff who had day jobs and of housewives who had children, because it was felt that the extra hour would be too demanding for them.

Complaints from the workers had no effect on the managers' decision.

Jed: 'They just don't listen, do they? I don't see the point of opening the club for an extra hour during the week. The weekend, yes, I can see the logic behind that. But it's just dead here during the week. Opening an extra hour won't make any difference. So we serve one more customer, so what? Anyway, if that's what they want to do, so be it, but surely it's not up to them to decide whether or not I can get up for work in the morning or whether or not I'll be able to make it here during the week, after work.'

Chris: 'Oh it's not fair, it really isn't. They know I need this job, well, let's face it, we're not working here for fun, are we?

Oh, but I can't not work and even though I don't really like it, it does help with the mortgage. Bloody managers, excuse my language, they think they're God, don't they?'

Deliah: 'Man, they ain't takin' my job offa me. I got my man to support. And the kids, they wan' all them latest things. Me bones they tell me somethin's goin to happen roun' this place.'

Deliah carried on in this vein for several days, grumbling about the managers and predicting that something was about to happen. When pressed to reveal what this might be, she was initially unable to answer: 'I doan' know, somethin' though.' Eventually this answer changed to 'Wait and see,' but that was all she could say.

At 1 a.m. the following Friday morning, while Deliah was off 'with a cold', something did happen. The managers and five strangers were observed to be searching the club. Eventually, it seemed that they had not met with any success. They stood together and had what appeared to be a very earnest discussion. As a result of this the General Manager walked away from the group, went onto the dance floor and then clambered onto the stage. Even though the band leader was in the middle of a song, it was obvious that the General Manager was asking him to stop playing. The General Manager said something to him and the band leader then asked everyone in the club to evacuate the premises. This, of course, caused a great deal of alarm among both the staff and the customers, who left the club as quickly as they possibly could. The rumour being circulated was that there had been a bomb planted in the club. Many of the customers decided there and then to either go home or go on to another club, as it would obviously take some time to search the whole building. Eventually it was decided that the telephone call had been a hoax, as no bomb was discovered.

The following evening when Deliah was back at work again and heard what had happened, she said, 'I told you that somethin' was going to happen!'

The irony of the situation was that the managers eventually decided that the staff they had intended to dismiss could stay.

Summary

Disruptive practices will usually be employed by staff rather than managers.

Disruptive practices are used to relieve boredom, to bring about change in a frustrating situation and to prevent staff from dwelling on the fact that they are in 'dead-end' occupations.

The fact that disruptive practices can have unpredicted and unsought consequences renders it less popular than other forms of defiance.

The motives for disrupting the workplace were mainly attributable to internal reasons and the preferred style was that of Rebel action.

8

MISUSE

When the Managing Director of Dairy Products Ltd discovered two red apples rolling about on the floor of the firm's Bentley he became very suspicious. His investigations revealed that Jones, the driver, was using the car to do 'odd jobs', because he was dissatisfied with the money he earned. In the last instance Jones had been helping out his nephew who managed a very large orchard. One of the lorries was out of action and so Jones had been using the Bentley to transport apples and pears. In return for this he had been given an unspecified sum of money.

With misuse, people attempt to get even by using the organisation's property and/or facilities for their own personal ends rather than the use for which the property and/or facilities were intended.

The six cases of misuse recorded at Alpha all involved the managers. Even though it was suspected that many more than this had occurred, a number of potential cases had to be discounted as the data we had was insufficient. The main barrier to the gathering of adequate data was that it was not always possible to have full access to the managers' activities. They occupied the night-club for many hours during the day and also spent a great deal of time in their offices, an area prohibited to staff.

Further, when it was realised that no cases of misuse were being recorded on the part of the staff this was initially something of a puzzle. However it became apparent that Alpha was not an organisation which would easily lend itself to misuse on the part of the staff. Access to the facilities which could have been misused, for example, those in the kitchens and offices, were restricted. Further, discreet enquiries revealed that misuse was low on the list of individual's priorities as a means of getting even. The staff believed that more satisfaction was to be derived from such things as pilferage or rule-breaking. However, in organisations where access to money and items which could be pilfered is severely limited or non-existent, misuse then becomes a more popular form of getting even.

Christmas cakes and mince pies

An employee of another much smaller night-club within IEC itself told us of a form of misuse which regularly occurred there. The manager was not authoritative and the bar staff had a virtual free access to the club's facilities. Like those at Alpha, the bar staff were generally disgruntled at the low wages they received. However, unlike the staff at Alpha they could not hope to make this up by either pilferage or receiving gratuities. There were only two bars and thus fewer customers and less money being handed over. In order to redress the balance the ladies among the staff would use the oven in the kitchen to cook their Christmas cakes. Each cake would need a whole evening to cook and so they would decide among themselves when they should each have a turn. Brenda, who also used to come to Alpha on her night off, explained; 'There's a beautiful smell wafting all over the place an hour after the cakes have started cooking. And when Christmas is really near we bring in our mince pies and whatever to cook. Last Christmas Minnie did the Christmas cakes for seven of the neighbours, as well, not bad is it? Mind you the manager told her off. Well she was overdoing it, wasn't she?'

The night watchman in another night club would use the facilities to attend to his personal toilet. 'He does everything but have a bath there. If he could fit in the sink he would.'

However, from the six cases of misuse which were recorded at the Alpha it was possible to determine that this form of getting even has certain salient features.

The consequences of misuse, as with inaction and disruptive practices, could not always be accurately predicted, as the case below illustrates.

Jumping chestnuts!

Doris, a barmaid, went into the kitchen to get some hot water to make a cup of tea. In order to reach the boiler she had to pass the deep-fat fryers. The General Manager and the Catering Manager were roasting chestnuts on the grill for their own consumption. As Doris was passing by, one of the chestnuts jumped off the grill and into one of the fryers. As a result her bare arm was splashed with hot fat and she was severely burned.

As time passed it was quite obvious that Doris was going to be scarred for life. She made a legal claim for compensation. Yet, despite the fact that she had witnesses to support her claim, the managers denied that they had been in the kitchen at that time and that they had been roasting chestnuts.

Doris, who claimed that she had been both physically and psychologically hurt, was disgusted with the managers at Alpha and the system as a whole which she felt had failed to protect her rights.

According to a reliable source the General Manager was heard to say, 'We'd have been in hot water if the top brass knew that we'd been in the kitchen roasting chestnuts. They'd have played merry hell with us.'

On occasions misuse can be used to get even in a substantial way, as shown by the following case.

Anthony the consultant

Anthony, a consultant, was fired on the grounds that he had been behaving dishonestly. Unabashed, he insisted that he should be allowed to continue to use his office and the firm's facilities until the last day of his employment. He spent the last week using the photocopier and contacting potential clients from all over the world. The itemised telephone bill for that last week alone was considerable. Anthony went on to set up a new management consultancy and offered clients from his previous firm a 30 per cent discount, for an initial visit. He also offered a 40 per cent discount if clients transferred their contracts to his new business. One of the directors of his previous firm said, with a resigned air, 'Anthony's doing very well, thanks to us.'

Unlike Anthony, most people who misuse their organisation's property do so on a smaller scale. For example, the school gardener who regularly takes the gardening tools to use on his own small plot at home; the hotel chef who does not have room in his small flat for a chest freezer and so makes use of one of the hotel's to store his own food; the taxi driver who uses his taxi to take his children to school and his wife to the shops.

And how many of us have made personal telephone calls from the office or used office stationery to write letters?

Misuse: Meanings and motives

Table 14

	Motives		
Misusers	P	I	E
Managers	5	1	0

P=Personal   I=Internal   E=External

Of all other forms of getting even, the organisation emerged as the main cause of discontented behaviour. Misuse was exceptional in this respect, in that it was personal motives which were mainly given as the reason for getting even (see Table 14 above). We found that the explanation lay in the managers' proprietorial attitude to the branch in which they worked. Their conversations and comments would be peppered with comments and phrases which suggested that they treated the building and the things which were in it as their own (see Chapter 3). Therefore, when they were using the organisation or facilities for their own ends, their attitude was that it was theirs to use as they saw fit. However, as will be seen in 'Styles' below, the fact that misuse was usually carried out covertly, indicates that their true position, that of employee, was never that far away from their thoughts.

From our research and experience, we suspect that in an organisation where the staff would have more opportunity than those at Alpha to misuse its property and/or facilities, and that if they did so, the organisation would be likely to come out on top as the main source of discontent.

The personal motives which the managers attributed to their actions were the desire for more status, autonomy and the relief of boredom. The case above in which the managers were roasting chestnuts was carried out in an endeavour to relieve boredom. In the following case the Catering Manager and his assistant were attempting to exercise their autonomy.

One evening Patrick, the Catering Manager, himself a relatively new member, introduced Stewart, his new assistant to the staff. They spent some considerable time that first evening standing at the end of the bar. It was a mid-week evening and therefore business was slack. Heather, who was working on that bar, could not help but overhear some of the conversation. It seemed that during the course of the night they discovered that they had certain mutual friends.

Christmas was three weeks away when Patrick told the staff that a party had been booked for the Sunday before Christmas. He told the staff that anyone who worked on that night would receive double pay, free sandwiches and a slice of gâteau. As he had most unusually given the staff sufficient notice and was, as Gina said, 'treating us like human beings for once', he soon had a contingent of willing volunteers.

The day of the party eventually came round and when the bar staff came into work it was to find that the kitchen staff had been very busy. Long tables had been set up and were covered in festive table-cloths and laden with a sumptuous feast.

The guests duly began to arrive and it soon became apparent to the staff that the guests were none other than Patrick's and Stewart's friends and relations.

It was the New Year before we learnt that Patrick and Stewart had managed to keep the General Manager in the dark. As far as he was concerned the people who had booked the party with Patrick had given a false name, false address and false telephone number. As Patrick had not been a Catering Manager for very long, he was not penalised for failing to ensure that the booking was made by trustworthy citizens. He was simply warned to be on his guard against it happening again, by taking the usual routine precautions.

Styles

Table 15

Style of Misuse	Trooper	Sniper	Protester	Rebel
Managers	0	0	1	5

As can be seen from Table 15, most cases of misuse involved Rebels. Both the Alpha cases described – those of the chestnuts and the party – were of this type.

Only one case involved Protesters, and in that instance all of the managers apart from the General Manager were involved.

The managers were dissatisfied because the General Manager had asked them to work extra hours that week in preparation for a visit from Head Office. One morning, seeing that the cleaning ladies had completed their work more quickly than usual, the managers set them to work cleaning their cars. When the General Manager found out what was going on and demanded to know the reason why, they told him that it was because they had recently spent so much time at Alpha that they did not have enough time to wash their cars.

At first glance, considering that the managers' attitude to Alpha was proprietorial, it might seem surprising that only one instance took place openly. If the managers truly regarded the Alpha as theirs why not always be quite open about using its property or facilities for their own ends?

The answer lay in their relationships with those who were subordinate to them and with those to whom *they* were subordinate. In their relationship with the staff and the customers of Alpha the managers were observed to play the role of owner/ manager. Conversations with the staff would be punctuated with phrases such as 'my bar', 'my staff' and 'my club'. However, this proprietorial attitude would be dropped in front of those who occupied higher positions in the hierarchy of the organisation. For example, in dialogues between the Catering Manager and the General Manager which were either overheard or reported, the Catering Manager would not speak of Alpha as 'his' in front of the General Manager. By the same token, the General Manager was observed to adopt a very deferential attitude to those who occupied positions in the higher echelons of the organisation. Therefore, while the managers might take on the role of 'owner' in front of their subordinates they were obviously ever mindful that to their superiors they were mere employees. And that their superiors would not look on them too favourably if they had reason to believe that the managers had been involved in a case of misuse.

Not only were most cases of misuse carried out covertly, but at least two managers would be involved each time. There were two reasons for this. Firstly, it was easier to plan and carry out a case of misuse if at least two people were involved. Secondly, these cases took place as a result of shared feelings or belief. In the case of the chestnuts the managers thought that the roasting and eating of chestnuts would be a pleasant diversion. And Patrick and Stewart believed that using Alpha to entertain their friends and relations would demonstrate the extent of their power and authority.

Summary

Only six cases of misuse were collected at the Alpha and these were carried out by the managers.

Their motives were mainly Personal and they preferred to take Rebel action.

While the Alpha did not prove to be a very fertile ground where misuse was concerned, it should not be assumed that this form of getting even is unpopular. As was explained at the beginning of this chapter, the managers were probably involved in more than the six cases of misuse. However, access to all they did and said was limited and thus only six cases could be adequately documented. Further, the property, facilities and organisation of Alpha were such that it was difficult for the staff to get even through misuse. Not only this, misuse was low on their list of priorities, as it was easier for them to get even in other ways. In organisations where employers do not, for example, have access to money, misuse, as a form of getting even, is likely to be much more prevalent.

REVIEW OF THE KEY POINTS

While acts of getting even may be carried out in many different ways, as we have seen in Part II, they all have certain key characteristics in common.

The aim of this review is to:

- Identify those shared key characteristics

- To compare getting even to more conventional forms of conflict-resolution

Action strategies

As shown in Part II, managerial and staff activities at Alpha were not limited to formally approved of roles and specified tasks. They exceeded the conventional domain and took part in a wide range of unorthodox activities. These activities could belong to any one of the six categories below:

- Pilferage

- Indiscipline

- Destructive practices

- Non-cooperation

- Disruptive practices

- Misuse of facilities.

These practices constituted the response of an individual or group to a particular situation. In engaging in these forms of behaviour managers and staff attempted to define, redefine, negotiate, alter, change or simply adjust to and cope with situations in the workplace. These unconventional actions also included many cases of managers and staff attempting to communicate, to partially resolve and to express the resentment that they experienced at work.

Styles

Not only could members of an organisation adopt any one of six action strategies to express defiance, but each of those six strategies could be carried out in four different styles:

- Lone Ranger – Individual-overt

- Sniper – Individual-covert

- Protester – Collective-overt

- Rebel – Collective-covert

The style adopted is determined by the intention of those involved: i.e., whether the individual wishes to act alone or in concert with others, and whether he/they wish to act overtly or covertly.

While conventional forms of expressions of discontent can take either individual or collective forms – strikes, quitting, absenteeism – they can only ever be, by their very nature, overt.

In contrast, the research at Alpha indicated that while acts of getting even are generally thought of as covert activities, they can be carried out both covertly and overtly.

131

Mediums for getting even

Anything within the organisation may be used as a medium for getting even provided that an individual or group has access to it: raw materials, finished products, production equipment, customers, other people within the organisation – the list is endless.

Potential use

Acts of getting even, whether covert or overt, individual or collective, are goal-seeking forms of behaviour. These goals fall into three main categories: facilitative, inhibitive or futile.

Solving a problem

In this category of facilitative purposes, the people involved are not normally attempting to get even. Instead, actions such as rule-breaking are employed to solve a particular problem in the workplace, usually difficulties associated with the processes of the work itself. The irony of this is inescapable.

Making life difficult

In this category of inhibitive purposes, individuals and groups attempt to make it difficult for others to gain their objectives at the expense of others. Unlike facilitative actions, those in this category usually are employed as a means of getting even. The perpetrators feel that their interests conflict with those of others to such an extent that they have to take action. Part II abounds with examples of this kind of workplace activity.

Getting mad

Futile attempts to get even are the most notorious. They occur when an individual or a group creates a situation in which neither they nor those they are in conflict with can achieve their objectives. Such acts of getting even can be described as the most primitive and childish.

While it is commonly believed that these acts are spontaneous, observation has revealed that futile attempts at getting even are often the last stage of a psychological process and are used as a last resort. Those involved may well have attempted to resolve their problems in other ways, perhaps by using facilitative or inhibitive forms of behaviour. Such a development could take hours, days or even months to come to fruition.

Tangible and intangible gains

Unconventional forms of behaviour, for whatever purpose they may be employed, usually provide their users with some kind of immediate and short-term gain. These can be tangible, intangible or both.

Tangible gains involved perishable or unperishable goods – money, raw materials, production equipment and even the personal belongings of those against whom the action is taken. Pilferage is typical of the kind of action which can lead to tangible gains.

Intangible gains can either be physical, social or psychological. A single action may lead to one or more of these intangible gains. The nature of the intangible gains will be directly related to the individual's view of what has been obtained, so that the same action may lead to different intangible gains for different people.

Rule-breaking, for example, may mean that one expends less physical effort at work by arriving late, going home early or by taking longer breaks. These same practices may also bring social acceptance from the individual's or group's peers. Additionally or alternatively, psychological benefits such as a sense of personal satisfaction, relief or achievement may be accrued.

Obviously, getting even may yield both tangible and intangible gains. Through an act of pilferage, for example, an individual may not only gain money but also a sense of achievement.

Unpredictability

Attempts at getting even are usually, though not always, carried out covertly. When attempts to get even *are* carried out covertly, the intention of the perpetrator(s) and the nature of the action may not be known to those against whom the action is taken. (The nature of the action may of course eventually be discovered but not until it is much too late to do anything about it.)

Unpredictability is therefore often associated with unconventional practices. Further, as recognised procedures for dealing with the expression and/or resolution of discontent in unconventional forms do not exist, actions are normally taken unilaterally and without either warning or an attempt to obtain consent.

Finally, there are so many factors involved in the inception and performance of an act of getting even that it is well-nigh impossible to predict exactly when and where these acts will occur.

Underlying meanings and motives

Attempts to get even are not aimless, irrational and impulsive. They are deliberate actions and inactions that are initiated by underlying motives and can be accounted for by the meanings advocated to them. In other words, attempts to get even have psychological validity for those who undertake them; thus

- All forms of unconventional behaviour are meaningful actions

- When they are employed to display resentment, they are also conscious and intentional attempts on the part of the aggrieved to express discontent with the party with whom they are in disagreement

- *Individual* actions, whether overt or covert, are based on unshared values, thoughts and beliefs, whereas *collective* action is usually based on shared or compatible values, thoughts and beliefs

We identified twenty-five different motives for attempting to get even. These are necessity, frustration, boredom, tension and stress, habit, fear, depression, ideological reasons, sheer bloody-mindedness, the need for security or to conform, the desire for enhanced status, the desire for greater autonomy, financial gain, facilitation of the work process, having fun, the urge to challenge authority, desire for more control over the work process, the desire to discredit another party, revenge, enjoyment of the sense of taking a risk, a need to maximise profits, anti-organisation feelings, or a sense of personal challenge (e.g. one might regard one's ability to pilfer without being detected as an achievement).

Whatever the motivation, observations suggest that attempts to get even will have one of these three main sources of motivation:

- Internal – i.e. the organisation itself, which is more often the case than not

- Personal

- External

135

Direct impact on the work environment

All forms of getting even will have either a direct or indirect impact on the organisation. The destruction of equipment or the pilferage of money or raw materials have an obvious direct impact on the organisation, while actions such as disruption which results in the loss of working time will have an indirect impact.

Unorganised and . . .

In contrast with conventional channels of conflict-resolution, the fact that getting even is an unconventional means of expressing discontent renders it organisationally and socially unacceptable. Destructive practices, for example, are commonly referred to as illegal, irresponsible, contemptible and criminal. However, while the unorthodox nature of the different forms of getting even prevents them from being *formally* institutionalised, they may sometimes become *informally* institutionalised, as in the case of the bakery worker who is 'allowed' to take home bread and cakes at the end of the day in lieu of better wages.

The frequency with which acts of getting even occur within the workplace is an index of conflict within the organisation. It should also be noted that attempts at getting even can occur whether or not there are formal procedures for conflict-resolution. If attempts to get even occur where institutionalised channels of conflict-resolution exist, it means that those involved do not believe that the problem can be resolved by these conventional means.

Ways of getting even will be employed in all organisations, whether or not they have been recognised and institutionalised as a means of resolving conflict.

Lastly, the fact that getting even is 'unorganised' or informal does not mean that it is necessarily '*dis*organised'. If a group chooses to get even they will have objectives, a choice of method, strategy and leadership, and they will allocate tasks and responsibilities and execute the plan systematically.

. . . Unresolved

As we saw in Part II, attempts to get even can only help to *mitigate* feelings such as frustration. They cannot go any way towards *resolving* the problem. This is because there are no institutionalised procedures for dealing with conflict-resolution by means of pilferage and other generally undesirable behaviour. And because such behaviour is viewed as socially and organisationally unacceptable, it is usually carried out covertly. So while the consequence of discontent can often be observed in the form of a particular action – money missing from a till, for example – the reasons for its genesis never come out into the open, and thus the problem remains unresolved.

This is in stark contrast to conventional expressions of discontent such as strikes, where there are institutionalised procedures for dealing with the conflict, and where the possibility that the discontent will be resolved *does* exist. Unlike institutionalised forms of conflict-resolution, getting even does not lead to:

- A long-term and satisfactory resolution of discontent

- The formulation of a mutually agreed body of rules and regulations

- Improvement in the relationship between employer and employee

Part III

Traditionally, attempts to get even have been dealt with at a superficial level and on an *ad hoc* basis. If the identity of those involved cannot be discovered, as in most cases of getting even, the management have to 'grin and bear it' and 'suffer in silence'. However, if the identity of the perpetrator is known, he can be instantly dismissed and even prosecuted, if the action taken merits this response. Indeed, at Alpha it was observable that the sacking of recalcitrant individuals appeared to be the only workable strategy by which managers could contain defiance at work. Yet despite the liberal use of dismissal and the occasional employment of scapegoating tactics, defiance was still rife. As one executive said, 'It's becoming more and more of a problem. We can no longer afford to ignore what's going on. It's time to face facts and do something about it. But what can we do?'

IEC executives are not the only ones who are becoming aware that acts of getting even pose a threat to the effectiveness and efficiency of their firms. Key individuals in many other hotel, catering and entertainment organisations have expressed similar concerns.

It is now gradually being realised that suffering in silence, varied by the dismissal and prosecution of staff, is not an appropriate managerial strategy, being inadequate for dealing with the various aspects of getting even at work. However, viable alternative approaches to undesirable activities within the workplace have not as yet been devised. Can attempts at getting even be dealt with adequately? We believe so, and we have devised a plan for positive action by which attempts at getting even in the workplace can be combated.

The aim of the plan is to create a 'total quality service culture'. On the strength of the substantial evidence available to us, this will substantially reduce both the desire and the opportunity to get even.

However, these proposals do not offer 'quick-fix' solutions. There is no short cut: getting even can only be effectively dealt with by applying, with a high degree of commitment, all the steps outlined in this chapter.

9

QUALITY OF SERVICE CULTURE

The hotel and catering industry is distinct from most other industries in its direct involvement with the consumer. Hotel and catering organisations can also be differentiated from one another in terms of the quality of service that each offers to the consumer. In our view managers should be concerned with creating a culture in the work environment that is conducive to a high quality of service. The creation of this culture will not only benefit the consumer, but will also reduce the desire and thus the attempts to get even. The means by which a high-quality service culture can be created are delineated below. We shall discuss the four elements of the plan for positive action. These are:

1. Reducing dissatisfaction at work

2. How to find out about problems

3. Give managers meaningful feedback

4. How to reduce temptation and opportunities to get even

1. Reducing dissatisfaction at work

All potential sources of dissatisfaction in the workplace can be allocated to one of the following four categories:

a) Bad working conditions

b) Lack of a comprehensive recruitment and training programme

c) Inadequate pay and reward systems

d) Inadequate supervision by management

The significance of these factors will vary from organisation to organisation. But even if you believe that, for example, working conditions are not a problem in your particular organisation, nevertheless bear in mind that working conditions are always a potential source of dissatisfaction.

At Alpha all four of the above factors were sources of dissatisfaction at different times and to varying degrees, and this inevitably led to dissatisfaction and a poor quality of service.

In service organisations the employee is more likely than the manager to receive direct feedback from the consumer. The consumer's dissatisfaction with poor service is reflected in his relationship with the employee. He can react to poor service by being abusive, over-demanding, merely uncivil and, worst of all in a low-paid industry, by withholding gratuities. The uncivil, non-tipping consumer can add to the frustrations experienced by the staff.

In order to reduce dissatisfaction in the workplace and thus to create a culture of high-quality service, attention should be paid to the four chief causes of discontent given above. In the following pages we shall indicate how these factors can be rendered not only less dissatisfying but transformed into positive sources of satisfaction within the workplace.

a) *Working conditions*

In service organisations such as Alpha, work units, including the kitchens, are often not specifically designed to ensure comfort, optimum productivity and quality of service. The following Action Levers can be operated against these problems.

Action Levers

1. Design and maintain work units according to the nature and requirements of the task in hand, the size of the workforce and the expected demand for services from the unit.

2. Optimise working conditions by providing adequate lighting, heating and storage facilities for service and production equipment.

3. Install essential support equipment (in Alpha, for example, equipment such as washing-machines, coolers, freezers, drink dispensers) and ensure that there are sufficient utensils, glasses and crockery for serving food and drink.

4. Allocate a common room, preferably away from the consumers, for use by staff and management.

5. Make the staff of each work unit accountable for its routine maintenance and presentation.

b) Recruitment and training policies

It is common knowledge that organisations in the hotel, catering and entertainment industries have a transient workforce, a high rate of labour turnover and a large proportion of part-time and unskilled employees. This means that:

- Most non-management employees see their employment within the organisation as a job rather than a career.

- Part-time employment often supplements a main income from full-time employment elsewhere.

- The seasonal and erratic nature of the demand for manpower makes it difficult to adhere to a long-term manpower policy.

- The unsocial working hours – early morning, late nights and weekends – coupled with low pay add to the unattractiveness of jobs in the hotel, catering and entertainment industry.

These difficulties place enormous constraints on management, and as a consequence:

- There are no coherent and comprehensive policies for the recruitment, selection and training of employees.

- The need of both staff and management for social and task-related skills in order to ensure a good quality of service is usually understated.

- Training is on-the-job and unsystematic, with little or no formal coaching from management.

- The costs of training are regarded as overheads rather than investments.

Consequently routine tasks are disrupted, and frequently so, when new employees are being trained. This inevitably results in a lowered standard of service for the consumer.

The following Action Levers can be operated against these problems.

Action Levers

1. Identify the seasonal peaks and slack periods and assess the manpower that will be needed over the long term – for the next year, for example.

2. As far as possible select staff on the grounds of task- and people-related skills, knowledge and experience.

3. Provide trainees with in-house but off-the-job induction before assigning them to their respective work units.

4. Allocate a 'coach' rather than a 'minder' to each trainee for a specified period of training.

5. Make supervisors responsible for monitoring the progress of each new member of staff and provide him with meaningful feedback on his performance.

6. Link training with rewards, bonuses, fringe benefits and promotional opportunities – for example, an increase in basic pay after successful completion of each stage of the training and development programme.

7. Provide follow-up training periodically and preferably for all members of staff.

8. The future training needs of the individual should be jointly identified by the individual concerned and his supervisor.

9. Train staff to function as members of a team.

c) Pay and reward systems

A key difference between the hotel, catering and entertainment industries and other industries is that a proportion of their employees receive not only wages but also gratuities.

They may also enjoy fringe benefits such as free meals and even accommodation. Gratuities and fringe benefits form part of what is known as the 'reward package'. Where there is little likelihood that the employee will receive gratuities, employers sometimes adjust the employee's basic pay accordingly. However, such adjustment of pay is the exception rather than the rule and certainly did not occur at Alpha. As a result, those who perform supportive functions, such as cleaners and glass-collectors, become dissatisfied when they compare their 'total reward' to that of their colleagues who work as bar staff or waitresses.

A further and general source of discontent at Alpha was that, unlike many other similar establishments, the staff were not provided with travelling allowances or arrangements to escort them home in the early hours of the morning.

Since the abolition of the Wages Councils, pay itself has been determined by employers using their own discretion as to what is fair pay for a day's work. At Alpha, the rate of pay and annual increments were fixed (non-negotiable) and were established by Head Office. Wages were not related to performance, the nature of tasks, the location of the organisation or the conditions under which an employee worked. At Alpha, as in many similar organisations, pay was according to the number of hours worked, and this payment system was one of the main causes of dissatisfaction amongst the work-force at Alpha.

A further source of discontent amongst employees was that they were not given extra pay for working overtime and unsocial hours. The managers, on the other hand, not only received a basic salary but also enjoyed a comprehensive package of fringe benefits such as bonuses, housing subsidies, car allowances and cheaper package holidays through one of IEC's subsidiary companies. Such differential treatment understandably became a major grievance amongst employees.

Employees' dissatisfaction over pay would be reflected in their relationships with the consumers. The fact that consumers can give employees tips, and do so if they are satisfied with the service, means that in effect certain sections of the staff – notably bar staff and kitchen staff – have two paymasters.

Gratuities can form a substantial proportion of an employee's earnings in hotel and catering organisations. A croupier revealed that his gratuities could be as much as ten to twenty-five times more than his basic earnings.

Bar staff will therefore quite often break the rule of 'first come first served' if they know or believe that a particular consumer will tip them for providing a fast and efficient service. On very busy nights, the bar staff at Alpha, who felt that serving everyone would be quite impossible, would concentrate their efforts on serving the regulars who were also tippers, and those 'strangers' who stood at the bar waving notes in the air and shouting, 'And one for yourself, when you've got a minute!'

The following realistic recommendations should reduce dissatisfaction with pay and reward and simultaneously improve the quality of service.

Action Levers

1. Do not use gratuities or other fringe benefits as an excuse for low basic pay.

2. Relate basic pay to responsibility and length of service with the organisation. Supervisors in particular should be paid more than those they are supervising. If they are also responsible for the training and development of staff they should also be paid accordingly.

3. Try to relate rewards to performance.

4. Provide a bonus system based on a periodic assessment of each unit's performance. This should include an assessment of the quality of service offered to customers.

5. Establish a 'pool' system to which each team member will contribute gratuities received.

6. Make each unit responsible for any losses or wastage incurred beyond an acceptable level (allowance should be made for genuine accidents).

7. Award weekly, monthly, biannual or annual certificates for quality of service to the unit whose performance and service has been exemplary.

8. Link the bonus system to the unit's output and to the quality of service it provides; and finally,

9. Ensure that the reward package is competitive in order to avoid the loss of trained staff to competitors.

d) Supervision

Interviews and discussions with managers at Alpha and similar organisations revealed that adequate supervision is usually understood solely in terms of establishing and maintaining control over the employees. This was particularly evident at

Alpha, where employees were simply expected to do as they were told. The importance of a suitable leadership style and a sound supervision network is not appreciated. In many organisations within the hotel, catering and entertainment industry there is a supervision gap between managers and employees.

At Alpha not all work units had the benefit of a supervisor, and where they did there was no guarantee that he would be qualified to occupy a supervisory role. The role of the supervisor would also be undermined by the desire, on the part of both the catering and general managers, to have direct and sole control over the staff. As a result very little respect was shown to the supervisor by the staff of a unit and this rendered the supervisor's task more difficult than it might otherwise have been.

A further and common problem, and one which is a major source of dissatisfaction in hotel, catering and entertainment organisations, is that a manager's responsibility for people and service and his formally authorised scope for action are not clearly defined. As a result, a manager in charge of the bars may interfere in the ways in which the activities of the box-office staff are managed. At Alpha, a multitude of problems arose from two causes. First, tasks were not properly planned and structured to ensure that overlapping between roles did not occur. Second, there was clearly a lack of respect for other managers' roles and their scope for action. This unauthorised supervision not only undermines the authority of the manager who is officially responsible, it also creates confusion amongst the staff concerned as to whom they are accountable.

Managers' narrow conception of what 'supervision' should entail, the weak position of supervisors (where supervisory positions exist), and the uncertain role-determination of managers provoke feelings of discontent and hence a poor quality of service.

The most significant action that can be taken to eradicate the problems of poor supervision, poorly stated roles and poor quality of service is to strengthen the role of the supervisor.

Strengthening the role of supervisors

This will require a major overhaul of the supervisor's relationships with managers and staff. These relationships will need to be restructured to achieve high-quality management, and traditional simple control mechanisms will have to be replaced. In order to obtain a high level of customer service, it is important to recognise and respect the sensitive and crucial role of the supervisor within the organisation.

Whilst the supervisor is accountable to the management, he should also receive a service from management in terms of support, both as an employee and as a supervisor. Management support for supervisors should be seen as a way of increasing the authority of supervisors. The supervisor will in turn provide a service to the staff over whom he is placed. The service offered to the staff will strengthen the trust relationship between staff and supervisor. Finally, the supervisor will also have to ensure that there is a high quality of service to the customer.

In short, the work-unit supervisor has to play a dual role. He has to become a part of the overall management team and simultaneously remain a team member of his work unit.

How can this be achieved?

Action Levers

1. Lay down a clearly defined scope for action for all the work units in your organisation.

2. Recruit a supervisor from amongst the members of each work unit. (New supervisory staff need to be recruited if a suitable individual does not already exist.)

3. Give the supervisor responsibility for the distribution and allocation of tasks, the coordination of work activities and the quality control of each unit's service and products.

149

4. Give the supervisor off-the-job training on team-building, people-management and the provision of prompt and high-quality service.

5. Recognise and be seen to recognise the supervisor's role as team leader and unit organiser.

6. Provide the supervisor with the authority to allocate resources as and when he deems it necessary, and support his decisions.

7. Place the supervisor in charge of a clearly defined work unit and make him accountable to his immediate manager.

8. Communications with unit team members should be conducted through the supervisor. Do not bypass the supervisor.

9. Recognise the supervisor's role as a two-way communicator between management and staff. This can be done by, for example, acknowledging suggestions made by or through him and by acting upon them if they are considered viable.

10. As people begin to feel committed to their work unit, involve the supervisors and unit members as far as possible in implementing viable proposals for the improvement of service quality and working conditions. Positive responses to the team members' requests, suggestions and innovative ideas will enhance the effectiveness of the team, the efficiency of the unit and the quality of service.

11. Acknowledge team and individual contributions to the attainment of the unit's goals. People are more enthusiastic when they see that their contribution to a particular reform or decision is recognised.

12. Ask the team to suggest a project that will solve a production or service problem. People derive great satisfaction from resolving problems.

13. Arrange periodic meetings of the supervisors and staff at which quality of work, quality of service, work-related problems and training needs can be discussed and future objectives can be set.

14. Arrange for the staff and supervisor of each work unit to meet regularly, preferably at the same time at the beginning of each week. While you should communicate your willingness to provide support, do not attend the meetings unless you are invited to do so.

15. Establish periodic meetings at which supervisors and managers can discuss the quality of the work units' service and products in relation to the overall effectiveness and efficiency of the organisation.

16. Progress made and resolutions taken at the meetings between supervisors and managers should be communicated to the members of each work unit by their supervisor at the unit meetings.

17. As staff tend to respect what is respected by their supervisors, managers should diligently attend the periodic manager-supervisor meetings.

18. People wish to know *why* they should do what is expected from them and how their actions will benefit them in their work. Explain the importance of regular attendance at the meetings.

How to create and maintain quality of service amongst employees and employers

Unfortunately, in most service organisations like Alpha service is regarded as something that employees have to offer to the customer in return for wages and other rewards. The quality of this service is controlled by the management to ensure that the prescribed standards are observed.

In contrast, in a quality of service culture staff are encouraged to think in terms of quality and to take action to improve the quality of their working life. The standards to be achieved are jointly decided and the necessary action is taken by *all* the people involved.

As for the managers in a service organisation, their prime function ought to be to ensure two things: first that they serve their staff, and second that the quality of the service offered to the costumer is guaranteed. In providing both internal and external service, management and staff work together to create and improve the quality of the service.

In endeavouring to create a quality of service culture it should be recognised that people are not likely to adopt new ways of doing things unless it is explained to them exactly what it is that they should do. Second, people do not abandon old ways of doing things unless they are convinced of the advantages of the new ways. Third, people are more likely to adopt new ways of doing things when they realise that the new behaviour is of benefit to them. Finally, as long as people's expectations are being fulfilled they are likely to remain faithful to the new ways of behaving. The increase in the quality of service offered to employees and customer will lead to an improved quality of working life experienced by those within the organisation. This will affect the way staff approach customers, and hence the quality of the customer–staff relationship will be improved.

Therefore, the following steps need to be taken.

Action Levers

1. Explain to staff what a quality of service culture is and what quality of service is all about.

2. Find out what the problems are and in what ways they affect the quality of work and quality of service provision in your organisation.

3. Find solutions for the identified problems of the work unit as a service team.

4. Review progress systematically and learn from your actions.

5. Help staff to think in terms of quality of service.

2. How to find out about problems

One of the action levers listed above recommends that in the creation of a quality of service culture existing problems within the organisation should be identified. Finding out what your problems are is one of the four essential elements of your plan for positive action – so how might it be done?

Attitudinal surveys

This method of data collection is used in many organisations nowadays to get people to tell us what is wrong with the present culture and the way in which their work is undertaken. Attitudinal surveys, of course, have limitations. Foremost is that they are usually most effective where large numbers of people are concerned. However, they are also an impersonal means of data collection and the quality of the responses generated is directly determined by the survey's design and by the respondent's attitudes to the use of questionnaires.

Meetings and quality circles

The supervisor–management and supervisor–work unit weekly meetings can provide an effective means of finding out what is wrong with the present system and how it can be improved. The most important condition is that people should trust one another and feel comfortable in putting forward ideas and solutions. At Alpha the monthly staff–management meetings were not productive. If the management were requested to provide assistance on the bars during peak periods or told that the slow service was partly due to the design of shelves which did not hold enough glasses, these statements were interpreted as criticisms rather than constructive suggestions. A once enthusiastic member of staff commented, 'We'd better keep our mouths shut. There's no point in putting forward suggestions when nobody cares.' It was generally felt that suggestions put forward by employees were not even considered, let alone put into operation.

To ensure successful quality circles, the following action levers can be operated.

Action Levers

1. Arrange for weekly meetings of the work units.

2. Create a favourable environment by encouraging staff and supervisors to participate in problem-solving exercises.

3. Encourage staff to contribute freely to the subject under discussion.

4. Record all suggestions and proposals and decide upon relevant actions.

5. Take action or explain why the action could not be taken.

6. Ensure that everyone in the organisation understands what quality service is about, what quality circles are and how they help to achieve objectives.

3. Give managers meaningful feedback

Quality circles and other means of collecting or generating relevant data cannot be of use unless the managers know how to appreciate and if possible react to feedback from lower levels of the organisation. Unless managers are sensitive to feedback from their staff, the creation of a quality of service culture within the organisation will be incomplete.

Action Levers

1. Train the managers to be sensitive to the information that they receive and to appreciate the contribution made by subordinates towards the overall management of the organisation.

2. Where possible, replace the assistant managers by supervisors and strengthen their role as team leaders of work units. This may not be applicable to large organisations.

3. Render good quality feedback available by
    a) Periodic work-unit progress reviews
    b) Work-unit weekly meetings
    c) Quality circles
    d) Informal discussion with employees

It should be repeated that, as we saw under 'Supervision', the single most important channel of feedback is the network of unit supervisors. It could be argued that in many organisations we visited a strong network of supervisors could have replaced an army of managers and assistant managers.

4. How to reduce temptations and opportunities to get even

Without doubt the practical strategies outlined above will help in the creation of a quality of service culture which in turn will lead to an improvement in the quality of service to customers, of the work itself, of work relationships and of the physical and socio-psychological environment in which service-related interactions will take place. It follows naturally that incidences of getting even will be substantially reduced. However, it would be unrealistic to expect managers to attain complete control of their employees' behaviour.

For example, improved manager–employee relationships will not always prevent pilferage when there are open cash tills. The very fact that opportunities to pilfer or to destroy equipment exist may induce the individual involved to express discontent by getting even rather than by the organisationally approved channels of grievance-handling. Preventative measures, specifically aimed at eliminating the opportunities for getting even, must also be employed.

Note that the practical guidelines provided below serve as supplementary managerial aids and need to be adjusted to the particular kind of organisation involved.

Reducing pilferage

Pilferage, as we have seen, is one of the most popular strategies for getting even at work and what is pilfered is determined by an item's usefulness and its accessibility. Items which are pilfered are either consumed (food or drink), used within the workplace, given to consumers free of charge or removed from the organisation. The aim should therefore be to reduce access to what is pilferable and the ease with which it can be consumed, given away or removed from the workplace. The following guidelines should help.

Any action will require initially that access to money and raw materials should be reduced as far as possible. The methods by which this may be achieved will vary greatly according to the organisation, and as we cannot hope to cover every eventuality here, the following suggestions are only intended to serve as pointers in the right direction.

In any organisation in which cash transactions take place between employees and customers, managers and owners should consider whether there are too many members of staff involved in this process, and if possible reduce their number.

If cash tills figure in the organisation, as in night-clubs, public houses, shops and restaurants, managers could periodically remove excess money from the tills, thus avoiding the build-up of temptation.

The use of cash tills with large and easily read display screens could also be useful, as even those customers who are some distance away from the till would be able to monitor the employee's actions.

If organsiations were to provide a secure room for the staff to leave their personal belongings, therefore eliminating the necessity for them to take cash, handbags or other personal items to the work units, this would in turn render it more difficult for organisational property to be removed in handbags and coat pockets.

It is also prudent to lock up as many of your organisation's materials as possible, so that only those who have legitimate access to those items can reach them.

Further, if stock controls were to be conducted as often as possible and at irregular intervals, this would severely hamper the well-organised operations that involve the loss of substantial amounts of money and raw materials.

However, a much more fundamental and effective method of reducing pilferage would be to involve the staff in setting up and monitoring a security system. Listen to the suggestions they make and if they are viable put them into operation. In this way the staff would become accountable for their actions and in effect become their own policemen. Individuals or teams in charge of production units could be given legitimate access to certain resources, those related to their particular unit, and rewarded in some way for good management.

You may also find it useful to seize any opportunity to strengthen the trust relationship between yourself and your employees. This may require a financial investment. In one night-club the Catering Manager instituted a 'Happy Time' hour, when the staff were served with food and drinks, at the end of the weekend session to encourage informal discussion of work-related problems with the supervisors and managers.

This strategy, we were told, had almost eradicated the unauthorised consumption of food and drink during working hours and had led to a substantial improvement in the state of the stocks.

There are also a number of activities that managers need to *avoid* in order to reduce the occurrence of pilferage.

It is always inadvisable to challenge your staff. For example, as we saw in Chapter 7, installing bright lights above the tills was ineffective as it only served to infuriate the bar staff. In another instance, the owner of a roadside cafe explained how he had riveted the metal ashtrays to the tables to prevent them from 'walking out' – only to find one morning that the tables themselves had disappeared.

Minimising rule-breaking

Observation suggests that the following categories of rules are the most likely to be broken.

- Vague and ambiguous rules

- Rules that are difficult to enforce and that require the voluntary participation of the people involved

- Rules that are devised to protect the interest of an individual or group interest at the expense of others

- Rules that are inflexible and restrictive in nature

- Rules that conflict with other rules

If any rule can be characterised by the descriptions above then it should be abandoned and a new one instituted in its place.

However, ensuring that rules are clearly defined, non-conflicting, just and flexible will not suffice to prevent them from being employed as a means of getting even. It is also necessary to ensure that every member of the organisation is aware of the rules and regulations and understands the reasons for their creation. *Communication* and *explanation* are the key words here.

It would also be beneficial to allow or even encourage employees to participate in rule-making and to welcome ideas for new procedures that might facilitate the work process. At the same time it would be expedient to identify and eliminate those rules and regulations that inhibit the work process.

Once employees have been involved in the process of revising, improving and devising rules, it follows that they should also be party to periodic examination of rules. A rule that came into existence at a previous consultation may in practice prove to be unworkable. Those concerned should therefore be able to modify, alter or change procedures if they need to.

Standard penalties need to be established and communicated to all members of the organisation. All rule-breakers should be seen to suffer those penalties, regardless of their rank or seniority. Again, it is suggested that the system of penalties should be arrived at jointly by employees and managers.

People who are involved in the processes of rule-making and the devising of penalties will naturally feel committed to observing those rules in whose genesis they have been concerned. Even so, every care should be taken to avoid the institution of rules which will be difficult to enforce.

Even when management and employees are involved in the process of rule-making, there may be occasions, depending on the type of organisation concerned, when managers may need to institute a new rule without first consulting employees. For example, lunch-times may need to be revised if there is a sudden shortage of canteen staff or a problem with food deliveries. In such instances managers should endeavour to avoid creating a situation of 'them' and 'us'. In the instance given above, it would be patently unwise to institute a temporary rule in which the management would have their lunch at

159

the normal time while the employees would have to wait their turn. This would be sufficient to create unrest and discontent in many organisations.

Finally, managers should refrain from using their prerogative to institute rules for the attainment of their personal objectives rather than of those concerned with improving quality of service.

Improving cooperation

Attempting to ensure that non-cooperation does not occur is far more difficult than, for example, securing cash or other valuable equipment within the work environment.

The preventative guidelines given above should be effective in combating most of the negative workplace interactions that result in non-cooperation. The improvement of workplace relations will substantially reduce the desire on the part of employees to fail to cooperate. However, given that cooperation may not always be forthcoming even in these circumstances, one can take some practical steps to enlist that cooperation.

The most crucial step is for managers and employers to recognise that, as we said in Chapter 5, when they are requesting employees to cooperate they should not ask them to do anything above or outside their normal work role. Managers and employers should bear in mind that as there may be times when there will be a need for staff to take on extra tasks, there will also be a need for staff to cooperate. Managers should prepare the ground accordingly. It is therefore important to maintain effective communication systems, both formal or informal, to ensure that everyone understands the objectives pursued by the management, whether on a regular or occasional basis, and the need for their achievement in relation to the overall effectiveness of the organisation.

Even though it may be difficult and perhaps time-consuming, it would also be politic to prepare for the unexpected by anticipating possible extra workloads and devising methods of dealing with them *before* they become a reality.

Once the stage is set, so to speak, there will be further steps to be taken when the need arises for cooperation from your staff. Your initial response should be to consider whether on this occasion there may be any grounds on which the staff may refuse to cooperate, and to attempt to resolve those problems before approaching the staff.

You should also consider whether or not what you are about to ask the staff to do is reasonable; if it is not, endeavour to temper the extra tasks in some way – perhaps by suggesting that once this particular objective has been achieved employees may leave work an hour earlier, with pay. When you actually approach your employees and ask them to cooperate, discuss with them in detail what needs to be done and explain the reason for doing it, and for doing it in the way in which you want it to be done. However, at the same time and if it is possible in your particular circumstances, you could ask for alternative ways of doing the job. If your staff can think of an alternative, evaluate it objectively and adopt it if it proves to be a viable proposition.

If you can, allow as much time as possible for the performance of a task. Most cases of non-cooperation were observed to occur when the time allotted for the performance of the task was limited. It may also be prudent to render individuals and groups accountable for that particular operation.

Finally, on the positive side, you should always bear in mind that you have asked your staff to devote extra time and energy to the achievement of organisational goals, and you must therefore show your appreciation by recognising the efforts and contributions made by individuals or groups towards completion of the task.

In our view the above guidelines are those that are most likely to be effective in ensuring cooperation from your staff. At times this may appear to be a lengthy process, and one that requires much effort on your part. You may feel tempted to take on a short cut and employ threats or punishment to ensure cooperation. However, as we discovered in the course of research, this often leads to non-cooperation and so should always be avoided.

Dealing with destructive practices

Clues as to how to deal with destructive practices can be found within the situations in which they occur. Remember that destructive practices are often employed as a last resort, are typically futile, and are usually undertaken by people who feel so outraged that they can either no longer think rationally or feel that other forms of getting even will not provide the satisfaction that they seek. People who resort to destructive practices are often unable to identify with the goals, objectives, culture, activities or leadership of the organisation. Any experience of discontent at work only serves to increase their feelings of isolation.

The psychological state of the individual or group that undertakes destructive practices can be best characterised as desperate and helpless. It is one in which people find themselves cornered, with no other recourse open to them. Destructive practices are usually the result of a prolonged and unresolved grievance that leaves the individual or group involved in a closed world of his or its own. The feelings of being victimised, that no one cares or that nobody is bothered typify the ideas that pass through the mind of the budding saboteur.

The likelihood of destructive practices occurring within an organisation will therefore be directly related to the management's ability to control the circumstances in which acts of defiance may take place.

First and foremost, attention should be paid to whether or not access to equipment and sensitive areas of the organisation is limited to authorised personnel. This may be the case in theory, but is it the case in practice?

Employing the practical guidelines given earlier will lessen the extent to which destructive practices are likely to occur. Communication, vertical and horizontal, needs to be improved. Supervisors, assistant managers and floor managers, who are regularly in contact with the employees and consumers, need to be exposed to sensitivity training and people-management. This will enable them not only to exchange information effectively but also to resolve minor grievances and problems that, if left unresolved, could resolve in frustration and the unnecessary mounting of tension.

When the channels of communication between management and staff are viewed as ineffective or blocked, it is vital for supervisors to be given the responsibility of liaising between the individual or group and management. Supervisors are in a position to identify communication blockages and inform the management of their existence. Of course, it is just as important for managers to listen to supervisors and pay attention to their views and comments.

Individuals will tend to feel less isolated only if they can identify with the activities and the objectives of the organisation. The phrases used by the management ought to be congruent with their actions. Use 'our' instead of 'my', 'we' instead of 'I'. People also need to be clear about the goals and performance of the workplace if they are to understand why they are asked to behave in a particular way.

Team development at the work-unit level would speed up the process of integration and improve work relationships. Individuals would be prevented from becoming isolated and would no longer have to face the burden of resolving work-related problems single-handedly.

Behind many cases of destructive practices lies a rigid managerial style for dealing with individuals who display work-related problems. Such an approach is likely to aggravate the situation. A more relaxed style of management would help to reduce the incidence of destructive practices. There are lessons to be learnt from those who adopt 'Management by Walkabout'

(MBWA) and an open-door policy. If grievances are addressed, even though not necessarily resolved, it helps people to feel that they have been 'listened to'.

It is indeed important to *listen* to people, even though you may feel that the account given is irrelevant or trivial; it may help you to expose shortcomings in the production or service network.

You should also avoid making unreasonable requests of your staff. This requires knowing the limits of their patience, tolerance or capabilities. Remember that 'the last straw' on top of a heap of problems may result in uncontrolled outbursts in which physical damage is inflicted on the organisation.

Finally, an effective managerial policy towards the elimination of destructive practices is, as observed in successful production and service organisations, that which *acknowledges* and *rewards* openness and creative and constructive behaviour. Only such enlightenment can ensure long-lasting effective and positive control.

Handling disturbances

Disrupting the work environment, 'creating a commotion', is done for a variety of reasons. The expression of resentment or frustration, relief of boredom, a desire to have fun or horseplay, release of tension and defiance of authority were amongst the most pertinent.

What do people hope to achieve by resorting to disruptive practices? Observation indicated that when in a work situation which was disliked and which employees were powerless to modify, alter or make more desirable permanently, they would attempt to bring about temporary change. These practices, therefore, are symptomatic of the presence of an irritating condition in the work environment and indicate that the need to deal with this situation has – for reasons of a structural or interpersonal nature – not been communicated to the management.

164

It is imperative to recognise that not all disruptive acts are carried out with the intention to inhibit target groups, for example management, from achieving their objectives. Nor are they undertaken as a futile exercise that would certainly not benefit those involved. On the contrary, as indicated earlier, it was observed on many occasions that most disruptive practices provided a feeling of relief and satisfaction for those who undertake them. In many cases minor acts of horseplay, which may even have temporarily disrupted the work and services, were ignored by the management. Why? Because most experienced managers see the need for livening up the often boring tasks.

A practical approach to combating these practices should therefore focus on the improvement of the quality of production and/or service processes and thus 'get the quality right' to start with.

Two major situations need to be addressed. Firstly those where, because of the low volume of work or ineffective distribution of the workload, some members of the staff have little or nothing at all to do. People do not like to be idle. They wish to be productive and get things done. When bored, either individually or collectively, they will attempt to change the circumstances which created the boredom.

The second category of situations are those in which as a result of too much work – demand from customers – staff find it difficult to cope and thus attempt to disrupt the situation. In a successful night-club with a very low record of cases of getting even, it was observed that the floor manager had asked each work unit to decide on the number of staff needed behind their bar, in the kitchen and so on, to enable them to cope with busy periods.

Therefore, if practical steps are to be taken in dealing with disruption, the following points need to be considered:

- Study the demand expected from each work unit and resource it accordingly

165

- Staff should be trained to service different jobs and activities so that when the level of demand falls in one area of production or service manpower resources can be utilised elsewhere

- If the members of each unit are involved in the process of determining the workload and which resources are needed, their participation will lead to them feeling committed to implementing changes in the work environment

Finally, when dealing with disruptive practices, it is essential to avoid dismissing them as irrelevant or as exceptional. Their presence in your organisation is symptomatic of a problem. It would also be imprudent to assume that only one individual is responsible. Group forms of disruptive practices seem to be preferred because of the common belief that there is safety in numbers.

Correct use of facilities

Our observations have shown that misuse may occur as an expression of discontent or because the people involved simply do not realise they *are* actually misusing the organisation's facilities. In many cases, at Alpha, the perpetrators of misuse when discovered would claim that they 'didn't know' or that 'I thought it would be all right.'

To reduce the probability of misuse occurring therefore, the first step is to ensure that all members of the organisation are fully aware of the proper use of its equipment and facilities.

Once this is established, it is probable that creating a quality of service culture will substantially reduce the desire on the part of the aggrieved to express discontent by means of misuse. For example, even though we did not observe that the 'them and us' regime accounted for cases of misuse at Alpha, this may simply have been because it would have been difficult for the staff to misuse the facilities and equipment to which they had

166

access. Our knowledge of other service organisations suggests that where employees feel that there is an unbridgeable gap between them and their managers and where they have access to equipment and facilities that could be misused, they will misuse them. If the above guidelines are followed the feeling of 'them and us' within your organisation should be reduced and thus instances of misuse will become less problematic.

However, as a further guarantee that misuse will not take place, supervisors need to be continuously supported by senior management so that there is greater positive influence over staff and their activities, or so that staff are rendered accountable for their own activities.

Finally, as stated in the early part of this chapter, policies regarding pay, incentives and fringe benefits should also be reviewed to ensure that an unbridgeable gap is not being created unintentionally between different members of the same organisation in terms of legitimate benefits.

Top executives and quality of service

Can the management of quality service be achieved without the involvement of top executives? The answer is simply, 'No!' Indeed, the initiative to create a quality of service culture should come from the strategic apex where decisions concerning overall policies and procedures are made. While it may be thought that branch managers are responsible for the creation of a culture conducive to quality, it is important to remember that managers in charge of branches, sites or businesses are themselves only part of a bigger picture. Managers are also employees whose quality of service to their staff will be determined by the attention given to their training and development by their superiors. Members of management need to speak with one voice and present a consistent picture in front of staff. For this, managers need to have the support of their superiors. If, for example, regional directors are not sensitive to the needs of the branch manager, it will be virtually impossible for branch managers to remove obstacles to the provision of a better quality of service.

As we saw in Part II, there were many occasions on which it was obvious that the managers at Alpha felt that the communication channels between them and the upper levels of management were ineffective. The managers would often use phrases such as 'my hands are tied'. IEC executives expected their managers to guarantee a high level of service to the consumer but could not see themselves as being a link in the long chain of service. As a consequence managers became dissatisfied and carried out acts of defiance. This in turn affected the quality of service.

In order to employ strategies which would create a quality service culture at the executive level:

- Top management must meet regularly to discuss their enabling contribution to the management of the workplace

- Top and middle management need to be clear that they are pushing the same consistent message down the line

- Top management need to find ways of motivating middle management to behave in a manner that is conducive to quality of service and total quality management

- It is vital to realise that management communicate most by the way they behave and not by what they say or write – so top and middle management must be able to identify consistent, positive types of behaviour and, if need be, give each other feedback on how best to achieve positive and consistent behaviour that is stimulating to staff within the workplace.

Conclusion

In conclusion, it is imperative to note that the plan for positive action offered here needs to be taken seriously. The four parts of this set of recommendations should also be assiduously applied. To use only one set of strategies – for example, 'Removing sources of dissatisfaction' – would be inadequate. If acts of getting even are to be greatly reduced or even eradicated, a high level of commitment and mutual trust will be required on the behalf of both employers and employees. As suggested, a new work culture can be created in which members of the organisation strive together to improve the quality of their work relationships and create a more productive and efficient organisation.

However, we should also like to suggest a further step. Managers, directors, owners and employers should not just be content with solving the problem of getting even in their own particular organisation. Throughout the course of this research we have come to recognise that a considerable amount of effort and planning is devoted to many acts of getting even. Spectacular instances of getting even prove that there is a vast amount of energy and resources within organisations and that it is only a lack of effective management that has led to it being perverted into unacceptable channels. But this need not be the case. Once getting even is effectively dealt with, as outlined in Chapter 9, the energy and potential inherent in each member of the organisation could be skilfully managed, developed and channelled towards improved productivity, a better quality of service and an enhanced quality of working life.

Understanding getting even at work is only the start of an intriguing journey, the end of which may bring permanent satisfaction and rich rewards.

INDEX

INDEX